Performance-Based Curriculum for Language Arts

From Knowing to Showing

Helen L. Burz
Kit Marshall

Performance-Based Curriculum for Language Arts
Performance-Based Curriculum for Mathematics
Performance-Based Curriculum for Science
Performance-Based Curriculum for Social Studies

Performance-Based Curriculum for Language Arts

From Knowing to Showing

Helen L. Burz
Kit Marshall

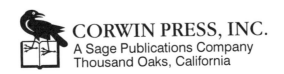
CORWIN PRESS, INC.
A Sage Publications Company
Thousand Oaks, California

For information address:

Corwin Press, Inc.
A Sage Publications Company
2455 Teller Road
Thousand Oaks, California 91320
e-mail: order@corwin.sagepub.com

SAGE Publications Ltd.
6 Bonhill Street
London EC2A 4PU
United Kingdom

SAGE Publications India Pvt. Ltd.
M-32 Market
Greater Kailash I
New Delhi 110 048 India

Printed in the United States of America

Library of Congress Cataloging-in-Publication Data

Burz, Helen L.
    Performance-based curriculum for language arts: from knowing to showing /
       Helen L. Burz, Kit Marshall.
       p.   cm. (From knowing to showing)
    Includes bibliographical references (pp. 91-95).
    ISBN 0-8039-6508-7 (cloth : alk. paper) — ISBN 0-8039-6509-5 (pbk. : alk. paper)
    1. Language arts — United States.   2. Curriculum planning — United States.
    3. Competency based education — United States.
    I. Marshall, Kit.   II. Title   III. Series
    LB1576.B949 1996
    372.6 — dc20   96-35195

This book is printed on acid-free paper.

97 98 99 00 01   10 9 8 7 6 5 4 3 2 1

Corwin Press Production Editor: S. Marlene Head
Typesetting: Birmingham Letter & Graphic Services
Cover design: Marcia R. Finlayson

TABLE OF CONTENTS

PREFACE

Traditionally, textbooks and curriculum guides have reflected a focus on content coverage. Districts, schools, and educational systems have looked to publishers to define, at least in general terms, *what* should be taught and the order in which it should be taught. The result has been to place an emphasis on what students need to *know*, often with little direction regarding the role of relevance and meaning for the learning.

The technological impact on society and a scan of future trends clearly delivers the message that just teaching information and "covering the book" is no longer a sufficient focus for instructional systems. Instead, instruction must go beyond the content taught and actively engage learners in demonstrating how they can select, interpret, use, and share selected information. Educators are quick to accept this shift but are faced with a real need for models that depict ways this might occur.

Performance-Based Curriculum for Language Arts provides a unique model for taking instruction from the traditional focus on content to a student-centered focus that aligns selected content with quality and context.

Because of the focus on content related to a particular content discipline, textbooks and curriculum frameworks and guides have had a strong influence on *how* content is taught. The result, often, has been to teach facts and basic functional skills in isolation of a meaningful, learner-centered approach. There has been no purpose in mind beyond having students know certain information and skills. These previous frameworks and guides have also separated curriculum from instruction and assessment. *Performance-Based Curriculum for Language Arts* offers a new organization and alignment of curriculum, instruction, and assessment around practical classroom application and does it in a way that readily allows teachers to use it.

Although not intended to be a complete daily curriculum guide, *Performance-Based Curriculum for Language Arts* provides a planning framework that includes numerous examples of performance-based language arts set in real-life contexts. The numerous performance benchmarks, at Grades 3, 5, 8, and 12, and strands can be used directly or as guides for customizing instruction toward relevant and meaningful application of important knowledge around critical language arts concepts. *Performance-Based Curriculum for Language Arts* can be used to guide the development of a language arts curriculum throughout a family of schools or by individual teachers within one classroom or by an instructional team.

The framework is divided into four major sections:

1. Introduction to *Performance-Based Curriculum for Language Arts*
2. The Content/Concept Standards for Language Arts and Performance Benchmarks for 3rd, 5th, 8th, and 12th Grades
3. Technology Connections
4. Performance Designers

The Introduction is organized around a friendly question-and-answer format. This section is central to the remainder of the framework and provides the rationale and organizational structure for the book. The introduction also contains a discussion of performance-based learning actions.

The Content/Concept Standards for Language Arts represent the best thinking of current national experts and provide the substance for each performance benchmark. These standards are organized by major strands within the discipline. Performance Benchmarks included in this section represent descriptions of what could be expected from a student who has a high degree of understanding of a content standard in a high-quality performance. For example, the student might be asked to solve a real-life problem or develop alternative solutions to an issue or question that requires a solid understanding of the content/concept standard at one of four developmental levels.

Technology Connections provide guidance for the application of technology in some manner to a performance benchmark. These strategies are appropriate for students who are accessing, producing, and disseminating information through technology.

The last section, Performance Designers, provides an analysis of the performance designer, which is a planning tool for teachers. It requires a focus on the key elements of content, competence, context, and quality criteria.

At the end of the book, design templates and reproducible masters (see Appendix: Blank Templates) provide practical tools that can be used to customize and create classroom instructional material that will empower teachers and students to be successful in "showing what they know."

ABOUT THE AUTHORS

HELEN L. BURZ

Helen L. Burz is a doctoral candidate at Oakland University in Rochester, Michigan, where she received her master of arts degree in teaching. She received her bachelor of science in education from Kent State University. Helen has taught at the preschool, elementary school, and college levels. She has also worked as a principal at the elementary and middle school levels. As an innovative leader in curriculum design and instructional delivery systems, she has led her schools to numerous state and national awards and recognition and was selected as Administrator of the Year in Michigan.

She has addressed integrated curriculum and interdisciplinary instruction for the Association for Supervision and Curriculum Development's (ASCD's) Professional Development Institute since 1985. Currently, she works as an educational consultant across North America, speaking and conducting training for future-focused, performance-based curriculum, instruction, and assessment.

KIT MARSHALL

Kit Marshall earned her Ph.D. at Stanford University in educational leadership in 1983 and her master's and BA at Sacramento State University in 1968. After teaching across all levels, developing state and national dissemination grants in innovative educational design, and site-level administration, she pursued further studies in organizational development and technology. She has received numerous awards for her work in restructuring curriculum, instruction, and assessment. Her book, *Teachers Helping Teachers*, published in 1985, was the first practical handbook for educators on team building and mentor teaching.

Currently living in California, Marshall is an international speaker and trainer in future-focused, performance-based curriculum, instruction, and assessment. She is CEO of Action Learning Systems, an educational restructuring company and President of The Learning Edge, a World Wide Web (WWW) site dedicated to networking restructuring schools and communities throughout North America

INTRODUCTION

Authentic *performance-based education* asks students to take their learning far beyond knowledge and basic skills. A *performance orientation* teaches students to be accountable for knowing what they are learning and why it is important and asks them to apply their knowledge in an observable and measurable *learning performance.*

This shift "from knowing to showing" means that everything we do—instruction, curriculum, assessment, evaluation, and reporting—will ultimately be focused on and organized around these learning performances.

Educators, parents, business and industry leaders, and community members throughout North America are coming to agree that students should be demonstrating what they are learning in observable and meaningful ways. However, we have all been to school. Generally, our collective experience of what school *is* has been very different from what we believe schools need to *become.* If we are to succeed in the difficult shift from content coverage to performance-based education, we will need to have new strategies for defining and organizing what we do around *significant learning performances.*

Performance-Based Curriculum for Language Arts has been developed to provide the tools and the structure for a logical, incremental transition to performance-based education. *Performance-Based Curriculum for Language Arts* is not intended to be a comprehensive curriculum; it is a curriculum framework. The various components of the framework provide structure and a focus that rigorously organizes *content* around *standards* and *performance* around *learning actions.*

IMPORTANT QUESTIONS AND ANSWERS ABOUT *PERFORMANCE-BASED CURRICULUM FOR LANGUAGE ARTS*

Content/Concept Standards

Where do the content/ concept standards come from for this framework?

This framework represents the best thinking of current national experts in the discipline of language arts. Although there is no official national standard for content areas, the National Council of Teachers of English (NCTE) and the International Reading Association (IRA) with assistance from the Council of Chief State Officers have demonstrated strong national leadership and influence that could form the instructional focus in a K–12 English and language arts program. These recommendations have been used to form the content/concept foundation of this framework and are identified as content/concept standards.

How are the content/concept standards organized within this framework?

The discipline of language arts is organized by major strands within the discipline. These strands are listed and described in Chapter 1. They are listening, speaking, writing, reading, and viewing and representing.

How do I know which content/ concept standards to focus on with MY students?

What students should know by the end of four levels, specified as Grades 3, 5, 8, and 12, is described at the beginning of each content strand section in Chapter 1. These levels are identified to highlight the specific developmental stages the learner moves through in school. A first-grade teacher should teach to the development of the concepts identified at Grade 3. A sixth-grade teacher should use the fifth-grade and eighth-grade content/concepts to guide instruction. A ninth-grade or tenth-grade teacher should use the eighth-grade contents as a guide and teach to the 12th-grade content/concepts.

These identified standards provide the content/concept focus for the performance benchmarks within the discipline and within the four developmental levels. Each major strand is identified by a set of content/concepts standards and is followed by four performance benchmark pages: one at each of the four levels—3rd, 5th, 8th, and 12th grade.

Performance Benchmarks

What is a performance benchmark?

In *Performance-Based Curriculum for Language Arts*, a performance benchmark is a representative description of what could be expected from a student who has a high degree of understanding of a content standard and can use that content standard in a high-quality perfor- mance. For example, the student might be asked to solve a real-life problem or develop alternative solutions to an issue or question that requires a solid understanding of the content/concept standard. If the students don't have the knowledge, they will not do well in the benchmark.

Each performance benchmark is designed to target a particular developmental level identified as 3rd, 5th, 8th, and 12th grades. Many students will be able to perform at a higher level, and some will perform at a lower level at any given point. Where a student is in the bench- marking process will determine where he or she is in the continuous learning process so characteristic of performance-based education.

What are the components of a performance benchmark?

Each performance benchmark has:

1. A **Key Organizing Question** that provides an initial focus for the performance benchmark and the content/concept standard addressed in the performance benchmark.

2. Performance-based **Key Competences (Learning Actions)** that specify what students need to do with what they know in the performance benchmark (refer to Figure 1.1, The Learning Actions Wheel, on page 6).

3. **Key Concepts and Content** from the discipline that define what students need to know in the performance benchmark.

4. **Two Performance Tasks**, or prompts, that provide the purpose, focus, and authenticity to the performance benchmarks. Having two tasks allows a teacher to ask for a group or individual performance, or even to ask for a repeat performance.

5. **Quality Criteria** or **"Look fors"** that precisely describe what a student would do to perform at a high-quality level on that performance benchmark. This component serves as the focus for the evaluation process. How well students can demonstrate what is described in the quality criteria informs the evaluator about continuous improvement planning goals for a student. The profile that results from an entire classroom's performance benchmark informs the teacher regarding next steps in the teaching-learning process.

How do I use the performance benchmarks to inform and guide ongoing instruction and assessment?

The performance benchmarks will:

- Organize *what* you teach around a clear set of content/concept standards for a particular discipline

- Organize *how* you teach by focusing your planning on the learning actions that you will teach and assess directly during daily instruction

- Provide you with specific targets for your instruction—you will teach "toward" the performance benchmarks

- Focus your students on what they will need to demonstrate in a formal evaluation of their learning

- Communicate to parents that there is a clear and rigorous academic focus to authentic performance-based education

The performance benchmarks are primarily for evaluation of learning, *after* the learning has occurred. The performance designer, on the other hand, provides the focus for quality continuous improvement *during* the ongoing daily instructional process.

Technology Connections

***How about a technology connection for* Performance-Based Curriculum for Language Arts?**

A number of performance benchmarks in *Performance-Based Curriculum for Language Arts* have a companion application that uses technology in some portion of the performance. If students are currently accessing, producing, and disseminating using technology, you will want to use or expand the strategies found in this section. These technology connections also serve as examples for teachers who are just moving toward the use of technology in their classrooms.

Computer Icon

If there is a computer icon on the performance benchmark page, you can refer to the companion page that will extend the performance benchmark to involve technology.

Performance Designers

What is a performance designer?

A performance designer is an organizer that is used to plan for ongoing performance-based instruction and assessment. The performance designer in *Performance-Based Curriculum for Language Arts* uses the learning actions and connects them to content, context, and criteria. The power of these learning actions becomes apparent when students begin to recognize and improve their competence with each new learning performance.

How is the performance designer used?

The performance designer can be used to organize student performances in any discipline and with students at all developmental levels and in all grades.

The sample performance designers provided can be used just as they are or can serve as a starting point for new designs.

You are invited to copy the blank performance designers in the Appendix for your own classroom use, or you may want to create a new performance designer that fits your style of planning and thinking.

How can I design performances for my students?

Performances can be designed by following the steps provided in Chapter 3 on performance designers.

PERFORMANCE-BASED LEARNING ACTIONS

Learning actions organize what the students will *do* with what they *know* in each performance benchmark. Performance-based learning actions are based on four important beliefs:

1.	**Learning is a quality continuous improvement process.**	Students improve their performance with any learning when they have multiple opportunities to apply what they know in a variety of settings over time. As students become familiar with and adept at using certain key learning actions, the quality of each subsequent performance will improve. Students will be *learning how to learn*.

2.	**Certain learning actions, or competences, apply to the teaching/learning environment regardless of the age of the learner or the content being taught.**	The five performance-based learning actions coupled with continuous assessment and evaluation are applicable to all ages and in all content areas. The current level of competence with these learning actions will vary from student to student. There will be a considerable range of competence with these learning actions even within a single classroom or grade level. The focus of improvement is on comparison to a learner's last best effort, not comparison of students to one another and not on the content alone. Performance-based teaching and learning will focus on what students can *do* with what they *know*.

3.	**Successful people are able to apply certain key actions to every learning challenge. These actions have similar characteristics regardless of the challenge.**	When students learn, apply, and continuously improve in the learning actions, they are practicing for life after they leave school. Schools must allow students to practice for the challenge, choice, and responsibility for results that they will encounter after "life in school" is over. The more competent students are with a range of these learning actions, the more successful they will be in dealing with the diverse issues, problems, and opportunities that await them.

4.	**The problem with the future is that it is not what it used to be.**	Today's informational and technological challenges mean that schools must restructure themselves around a different set of assumptions about what students need to *know* and be able to *do*. Many educators and parents are reaching the conclusion that much of the information we ask students to remember and many of the skills we ask them to practice may no longer be appropriate or useful by the time they leave school. At this point, we ask the question, "If covering content is not enough anymore, what *should* schools be focusing on?" We believe the answer is "The learning actions."

THE PERFORMANCE-BASED LEARNING ACTIONS WHEEL

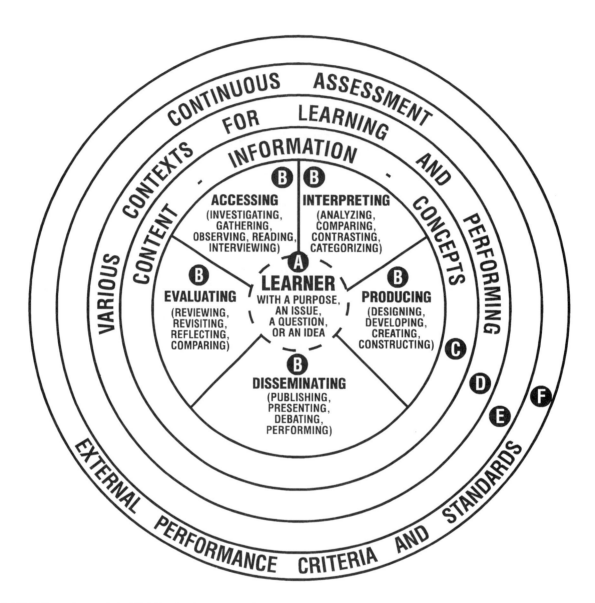

FIGURE 1.1 THE LEARNING ACTIONS WHEEL

Ⓐ The Learner

The learning actions are learner centered and brain based. At the center of the Wheel in Figure 1.1 is the learner with a stimulus for learning. That stimulus may be an issue, idea, or question that may have been suggested to the teacher by the content standards, or it may be something of particular interest to the learner. The learner is in the center because no matter how important we think the content is, it is inert until we add action to it. Everything "revolves" around the developmental levels, the motivation, and the engagement of the learner in the learning actions.

B The Five Major Learning Actions of a Performance

The learning actions include five major stages that learners will move through during any performance process. Let's look at the meaning and importance of each.

Accessing *What do I need to know?* *How can I find out?*	A performance begins with an issue, a problem, or interesting "lead." The learner accesses the information he or she needs to have in order to successfully perform. This information can come from a variety of experiences—but it must come from somewhere. Traditionally, information has come solely from the teacher or the next chapter in a textbook. In today's information-based environment, students must be adept, self-directed learners, determining what is needed and having a wide range of competences for accessing critical information and resources. Learners may investigate, gather, observe, read, and interview, to name a few actions. Whatever actions they engage in to find out what they need to know, *relevant* information must be accessed if the performance is to be as powerful as possible. Accessing is an important first step to a performance and a critical component of success as a learner in any role in or outside school.

Interpreting *What does all of this mean?* *So what?*	Critical reasoning, problem finding and solving, decision making, and other similar mental processes are what we must do as a part of any important learning that we intend to use in some way. Here, we must make sense of the information we have accessed and decide which information to keep, expand on, or ignore. This component of a performance asks us to analyze, compare, contrast, and categorize—to somehow meaningfully organize the information to represent what we think it all means. This component is critical to a performance process. It clearly determines the level of sophistication and competence with which we can deal with the amount of information constantly vying for our attention and time both in and outside a formal learning situation.

Producing
 	
*How can I show what
   I know?*
 	
*What impact am
   I seeking?*
 	
Who is my audience?
	The producing component of a performance is when we translate what we have learned into a useful representation of our learning. What gets produced represents a learner's competence with design, development, creation, and construction—something tangible that pulls the learning together in some form. This component is the acid test of a learner's competence as a quality producer, a critical role for working and living in the 21st century. In life after school, what we produce usually has a focus, an audience in mind. A powerful performance will always have a clear purpose in mind, a reason for the performance, and an impact that is desired as a result of the performance.

Disseminating

What is the best way to communicate what I have produced?

How can I impact this audience?

How will I know that what I've produced has had an impact?

The fourth learning action of the performance process is disseminating. At this point, we are asking the learners to communicate what they have learned and produced to someone, either directly or indirectly. This is also where the value of an authentic context, someone to be an involved and interested audience, is so apparent. Only in school does there seem to be a lack of attention paid to such a critical motivation for learning and demonstrating. This is truly the point at which learners are dealing with the challenges of a performance setting. Students may publish, present, debate, or perform in a variety of fine and dramatic arts activities, to name a few possibilities. Service learning projects, community performances, and a variety of related school celebrations of learning are all ways for the learning to hold value that may not be inherently present in the simple existence of content standards.

Evaluating

How well did I do?

Where will I focus my plans for improvement?

The evaluation component represents the culmination of one performance and perhaps the launching of another performance cycle. It is the point at which a judgment is made and plans are developed for improvement next time. The quality criteria (in the performance benchmarks) for all the learning actions are the guides for these evaluations. The performance benchmarks in this framework represent the personal evaluation component of ongoing learning and performing on a day-to-day basis, or the self-efficacy of the learner.

ⓒ Content–Information–Concepts

The learning actions are applied to the content–information–concepts identified by the educational system as being essential. Addressing information that is organized around major concepts allows the learner to work with a much broader chunk of information. Thus the learner is afforded the opportunity for making more connections and linkages and developing greater understanding.

In this text, the selected information has been aligned with the best thinking of current experts representing the National Council of Teachers of English and the International Reading Association, with assistance from the Council of Chief State School Officers.

ⓓ Various Contexts for Learning and Performing

A context for learning refers to the setting in which the learning occurs, or the audience or recipient of the fruit of the learning or the situation—any of which create a reason, purpose, or focus for the learning.

Traditionally, the context for learning for students has been alone in a chair at a desk in a classroom. However, the context can be a river or stream that runs through the community. Students working in groups with engineers from a local plant can be engaged in collecting specimens and conducting experiments from the water to determine effects of manufacturing on the water's purity, so they can submit a report to the company or the Environmental Protection Agency.

E Continuous Assessment

The continuous assessment portion of the learning actions wheel represents the continuous improvement process that is imbedded throughout each of the other components. An authentic learning community will engage in a supportive improvement process that is less competitive than it is collaborative and cooperative. To *assess* originally meant to sit beside. During key points in each component of the performance process, students will reflect upon their own work and the work of others. The role of the teacher in this process is to ask questions that guide the student's self-assessment and provide specific feedback to the learner about what is being observed. The conditions we create for this reflective assessment on a daily basis will determine the ultimate success students will have with the performance benchmarks.

F External Performance Criteria and Standards

The outermost circle represents the system's standards and scoring or grading procedures and patterns.

Remember, there are four critical components of a performance. The learning actions represent an organizing tool for a performance. They describe the components of the performance process. The learning actions also represent quality work according to identified criteria. By themselves, the learning actions are of little use. You have to *know* something to *do* something with it. In *Performance-Based Curriculum for Language Arts*, each performance benchmark combines all four components of a performance:

1) Content–information–concepts
2) Competence: learning actions performed by the learner
3) Contexts that create a reason and a focus for the performance
4) Criteria that define a quality performance

1
CONTENT/CONCEPT STANDARDS FOR LANGUAGE ARTS

WHY IS LANGUAGE IMPORTANT?

Language sets us apart from all other forms of life and makes us truly human. It is language that shapes our thoughts and our thoughts that shape language. Language is integral to all learning that takes place in school; it is the centerpiece of education. It is the means by which students assimilate their experiences and give meaning to those experiences. It is through language that students discover and learn about themselves and the world at large. It is language that causes students to affirm who they are and become part of a larger cultural community. The curriculum area devoted to the development and mastery of students' language in school is called language arts.

WHAT ARE THE LANGUAGE ARTS?

Listening, speaking, writing and reading are the four strands that educators have traditionally held central to the language arts. However, as we continue to move into the technoinformation age it is essential that we also consider the importance of viewing and representing as key components of the language arts. In a "media" society, viewing is primarily concerned with making sense of messages in visual texts, whereas representing refers to the production of visual or audio texts. Both involve the examination of relationships among audiences and texts, and how those texts are constructed.

Each of the strands is central to learning and expressing knowledge in all disciplines. Literature and the study of the English language are often considered part of the language arts, and they are. But they should not be taught in isolation from listening, speaking, writing, reading, and viewing and representing.

WHY DO WE STUDY THE LANGUAGE ARTS?

We study the language arts because they are integral to everything we do, every activity we undertake, every relationship we enter into, and every learning action in which we engage. Without the language arts, without the ability to communicate, without the ability to interpret — to make, convey and receive meaning, — we could do nothing. Our existence, culture, and sense of being, not just our learning, are bound together by listening, speaking, writing, reading, and viewing and representing. All of these language skills are equally important. They are interconnected, and a student's progress in one area influences and is influenced by development in the other areas.

Students are most likely to develop language competence, as well as thinking and social skills, when they have opportunities to use language to communicate for real purposes and in real situations, both in the academic context of the classroom and in the context of the broader community. Students will pass through the same stages of language development, but they may differ in their pace and ways of learning. The language arts program should recognize, respect, and value each student's developmental pace, as well as his or her racial, cultural, and linguistic background. This approach helps develop a positive sense of self and supports the learning process.

The goal of language arts instruction is to develop students who are effective communicators and thinkers, which means they will be competent listeners, speakers, writers, and readers, as well as viewers and representers. To achieve this goal, students must listen, speak, write, read, view, and represent in meaningful authentic contexts at every grade level in all disciplines.

INSTRUCTIONAL ISSUES IN LANGUAGE ARTS

Students learn language skills best when they use them in a whole, meaningful, and functional context, not through isolated exercises. In classrooms where language arts are integrated, students are working cooperatively, talking, listening, reading, and writing with their peers and outside experts. Language skills and strategies, such as spelling, grammar, usage, and vocabulary, are taught within the context of students' reading, writing, conversations, and creative experiences. Students need to write, read, and create in a variety of genres representative of diverse cultures—novels, memos, editorials, poems, films, television newscasts, reports, play scripts, journals, brochures—about topics that concern or interest them, and make meaningful connections between their learning in language arts and in other disciplines. Through these texts and various contexts, students learn to understand and appreciate their individual cultural heritage and the rich, diverse shared cultural heritage of our society.

In this technoinformation age, students need to develop the skills required to locate, interpret, and critically respond to information in various forms of print and nonprint media. *Media* is a global term that includes all forms of communication. This is where attention must be given to viewing and representing. *Viewing* includes not just the act of looking at a media product but also the entire range of critical and analytic activities required. *Representing* refers to the production of visual or audio texts and involves the examination of the relationships among audience and texts, and how those texts are constructed.

It is important for students to have opportunities to view material that expresses different perspectives and to learn to analyze the biases that are sometimes inherent in a production. Issues such as stereotyping, power, ownership, and accuracy need to be addressed. Analysis of media texts is most effectively done when students have an opportunity to construct their own texts. Through the use of production strategies, students will recognize the control the producer has over the many messages, explicit and implicit, that are conveyed.

Students need to be critical viewers and critical consumers of media texts. Acquiring the ability to understand, evaluate, and create a wide variety of media texts is an important part of language development. It is essential for students to be able to interpret information presented visually, orally, and electronically in order to see how it can shape reality. It is also essential for students to identify the viewpoint and biases of its creator and to decide whether or not they agree with that viewpoint. Likewise, students need to understand how to use the various media in order to communicate their own ideas and points of view.

LANGUAGE ARTS STRANDS

The six strands that make up the language arts curriculum, **listening, speaking, writing, reading, viewing,** and **representing**, are processes that students develop throughout their lives. These processes remain the same for all grade levels. What changes with every grade level are the degrees of difficulty of the materials, the difficulty of the tasks that students encounter, and the increased complexity and intensity of students' involvement and responses. In this document, the content/concept standards for each strand define what all listeners, speakers, writers, readers, viewers, and representers should be able to do. These content/concept standards are followed by developmentally appropriate performance benchmarks for Grades 3, 5, 8, and 12.

PERFORMANCE BENCHMARK FORMAT

The performance benchmarks are sample demonstrations designed with content, competence, context, and criteria that students should accomplish individually and collaboratively by the end of identified grade levels. For each of the seven strands, there will follow four performance benchmarks. There will be one benchmark for each of the following developmental levels: 3rd, 5th, 8th and 12th grade. Because these benchmarks represent different developmental levels, they should serve as guides for all teachers from kindergarten through 12th grade. The performance benchmarks are designed to represent a description of what could be expected from a student in a high-quality performance who has a high degree of understanding of the specific content/concept standard and has consistently experienced the learning actions.

The following template, along with descriptions, is offered as an advance organizer for the performance benchmarks that follow in the next section.

PERFORMANCE BENCHMARK FORMAT

A. LANGUAGE ARTS STRAND AND STANDARD NUMBERS		G. TECHNOLOGY ICON	
B. KEY ORGANIZING QUESTION:			
C. KEY COMPETENCES	**D. KEY CONCEPTS AND CONTENT**	**E. PERFORMANCE TASKS**	
		PERFORMANCE TASK I:	
		PERFORMANCE TASK II:	
F. QUALITY CRITERIA: "LOOK FORS"			

A. Language Arts Strand and Standard Numbers

This section serves to identify the selected language arts strand and the specific standard numbers chosen from the content/concept standards pages that precede each set of benchmarks.

B. Key Organizing Question

Each performance benchmark addresses specific content information and is organized around a key organizing question. This question serves as a focusing point for the teacher during the performance. The teacher and student can use these questions to focus attention on the key concept/content and competences required in the performance task.

C. Key Competences

The key competences represent the major learning actions of accessing, interpreting, producing, disseminating, and evaluating. These major learning actions are discussed in detail on the preceding pages.

The actions identified are what the student will *do* with the key concepts and content in this benchmark performance. Those do's or learning actions engage students in demonstrations of competence in technical and social processes. Teachers must teach students how to operationalize these learning actions.

D. Key Concepts and Content

The information contained in this section identifies the major concepts that embrace the essential content and knowledge base that was taught and is now addressed in this performance benchmark. These concepts correspond to the standard numbers in Section A above.

E. Performance Tasks

Each performance task requires students to apply the designated content using specific learning actions they have been taught. This is done in a context or situation related to the key question. The performance tasks can be done individually or collaboratively. In either case, it is still the teacher's responsibility to look for the presence or absence of the quality criteria in action.

There are two performance tasks identified on each performance benchmark page to offer teachers a choice or serve as a parallel task for students. Both tasks correspond to the identified quality criteria.

F. Quality Criteria: "Look fors"

The quality criteria represent key actions that students are expected to demonstrate during the performance task. The criteria also guide the teachers and serve as "look fors" during the performance task. In other words, the teacher observes the students for these specific criteria.

These criteria embody the key competences or learning actions that students should have been taught in preparation for this performance task. Students demonstrate the learning actions in connection to the key concepts.

The criteria serve as a process rubric that guides the design of both instruction and assessment. They also serve as a signpost for the learners.

The criteria are identified following a do + what formula, which makes it easy to "look for" them.

G. Technology Icon

 The presence of a technology icon at the top of a performance benchmark page means there is a corresponding example in the Technology Connections section. These examples indicate how technologies can assist students in carrying out the key competences required in the performance task.

LISTENING

Content/Concept Standards

Listening and speaking are the primary means of language learning, and they provide an essential foundation for all of learning. Students spend more time listening than they do reading, writing, or speaking, and as our society becomes increasingly media oriented, listening becomes more important as a language skill. Effective listening provides students with the means to explore a wide range of relationships, attitudes, ideas, and emotions. It is essential that we focus on improving listening literacy. Because listening is an integral part of every other activity included in the language arts curriculum, opportunities to teach listening skills abound.

Instructional Issues in Listening

Listening skills are not automatic. They must be taught. Instruction in listening should assist students in listening critically and appreciatively in order to interpret, evaluate, and integrate what they hear. Listening instruction should also develop students' ability to listen for information and concentrate on what is being said. Students should be able to listen with perception and understanding, and play an active part in the communication process.

Listening Strategies

Listening strategies are best taught when they are integrated into all the areas of the curriculum and when students are given many opportunities to apply those skills. Efficiency in the other language arts of speaking, writing, and reading increases in direct proportion to students' listening ability.

What all listeners should know and be able to do

Perceive and discriminate among sounds and visual images:
- Discriminate between sounds in language
- Identify letter/sound combinations
- Identify patterns in communication

Attend to the message:
- Concentrate on the message and the speaker
- Apply the different functions of listening: to imagine, for information, to assess and evaluate, for pleasure
- Respond appropriately and suspend judgment; empathize with the speaker using nonverbal cues

Assign meaning to symbols to interpret or understand the message:
- Identify the main idea and supporting details in an oral message
- Recognize organizational patterns: chronological, topical, spatial, comparison and contrast, problem-solutions, climactic
- Interpret spoken messages
- Determine meaning and sequence using verbal and nonverbal cues

Evaluate the message:

- Discriminate between significant and insignificant information, facts and opinions, relevant and irrelevant data, complete and incomplete messages, clear and unclear messages, and double meanings
- Keep an open mind; avoid jumping to conclusions

Respond to the message:

- Attend to the speaker
- Get and give feedback by questioning the presenter
- Review the meaning of the message by using interpersonal skills
- Time responses to reflect a sensitivity to the communication process
- Summarize the received information

Remember the message:

- Take notes to record current information, retrieve prior knowledge, and link old information with new
- Retain messages by using memory techniques: grouping, ordering, mnemonics
- Review notes at a later time
- Apply received information appropriately

The listening strategies are integral to the following performance benchmarks for each grade level.

What students should know how to do by the end of Grade 3

Students learn to listen purposefully in a variety of situations that enable them to receive and respond to information. They are able to listen for increasingly longer periods of time to stories and multimedia presentations and can recall important details and ideas. They follow oral conversations and are increasingly aware of the value of listening as a source of information and enjoyment. They discuss their roles as listeners and become more active participants in the listening process. They should be able to

1. Listen to literature and relate meaning and appreciation
2. Listen to questions and answer them effectively
3. Summarize what has been heard
4. Demonstrate a procedure that has been heard
5. Follow spoken directions
6. Retell what has been heard
7. Listen and speak in order to discover, discuss, and clarify new concepts and experiences; express preferences; and indicate interests in the various content areas

What students should know how to do by the end of Grade 5

Students enjoy listening and respond appropriately in various situations. They are aware of the importance of listening and can adjust their listening to fit the purpose. They increase their ability to listen critically and attentively to spoken messages by interpreting nonverbal cues, following the sequencing of ideas, detecting mood, asking relevant questions, and interpreting meanings of words. They should be able to

1. Listen to a speaker and ask appropriate questions about what was heard
2. Draw conclusions about what was heard
3. Complete a self-evaluation of listening behavior and skills
4. Distill key information from a presentation or conversation
5. Predict logical outcomes based on information given in conversation, discussion, or oral presentations
6. Clarify meanings of messages communicated across language or dialect barriers by using appropriate questions, paraphrases, and gestures
7. Record notes during a speech or lecture

What students should know how to do by the end of Grade 8

Students develop their listening skills at three levels: the physiological, the processing, and the interpretive. They require sophisticated skills at all three levels if they are to learn and benefit from the vast amount of multimedia material to which they are exposed. They must listen with sensitivity, understanding, and discrimination and develop proficiency in being a listener in conversation and discussion as well as a speaker. Students listen and respond thoughtfully and empathetically to a range of messages conveyed by others. They should be able to

1. Analyze a variety of speeches for determining main ideas, organizational patterns, and significant and insignificant information
2. Analyze television and radio transmissions including newscasts, advertising, drama, comedy, educational programs, teenage and children's programming, and so on
3. Compare and contrast points of view
4. Identify major propaganda techniques used in speeches and media
5. Interpret meanings implied by a speaker's choice and use of language and nonverbal cues
6. Recognize the emotional tone and appeal of a speaker's message
7. Detect logical inconsistencies in a speaker's message
8. Verify a speaker's information or expertise by using appropriate resources and procedures

What students should know how to do by the end of Grade 12

Students listen critically and appreciatively in order to interpret, evaluate, and integrate what they hear. They develop greater ability to concentrate on what is being said to them to the point where they are able to listen with perception and understanding and play an active part in the communication process. Students make value judgments regarding a speaker's information, qualifications, intentions, presentations, ideas, and persuasive effects. They should be able to

1. Analyze recorded passages from literature
2. Analyze and evaluate public speakers, speeches, and media presentations
3. Collect information and accomplish a variety of complex tasks by listening
4. Identify and evaluate the salient points or features of a speech or presentation

Language Arts:
Grade 3

Performance
Benchmark

LISTENING
CONTENT/CONCEPT STANDARDS 1, 3

KEY ORGANIZING QUESTION:

What did I hear?

KEY COMPETENCES	KEY CONCEPTS AND CONTENT	PERFORMANCE TASKS
Listen Summarize Compare Contrast Evaluate Design Develop	Comprehend and summarize oral messages.	**PERFORMANCE TASK I:** As a quality listener, you hear the teacher read you two different versions of "The Three Little Pigs" or some other story that is told from two different points of view. Listen carefully to what is read. Make a list of the main ideas for each version. Create a Venn diagram showing the features these stories have in common and those that are unique to each story. Compare your diagram with the diagrams of three other students in your class. How are they alike? How are they different? How can you use the new information to improve your diagram? Present your final diagram to another team in your class. Ask them what they learned. **PERFORMANCE TASK II:** Your class is going to visit another classroom as storytellers. In preparation for this event, you have been listening to stories read to you by your teacher. Now you must choose one. Practice telling it with expression. Tell your story and record it. Listen to your recording. Ask three other friends to listen to your recording. Ask them what you can do to make it more interesting. Compare their responses. Decide what changes you will make to your storytelling to make it more interesting for your audience. Make the changes and record it again. Listen, make final changes, and then present it to a new team of three friends.

QUALITY CRITERIA:
"LOOK FORS"

• Listen attentively.
• Interpret key points.
• Categorize the information.
• Compare and contrast responses.
• Summarize results.
• Compare with others.

Language Arts:
Grade 5

Performance
Benchmark

LISTENING
CONTENT/CONCEPT STANDARDS 1, 2, 4

KEY ORGANIZING QUESTION:

How does questioning help you gain information?

KEY COMPETENCES	KEY CONCEPTS AND CONTENT	PERFORMANCE TASKS
Listen Interpret Evaluate Question Conclude Create	Comprehend a speaker. Question a speaker. Draw conclusions.	**PERFORMANCE TASK I:** Your class has just had a Young Author's Conference during which all students in your class shared how they wrote their books. You must now ask one of these authors follow-up questions. List the questions you will ask. Following the discussion, write what you heard the author say about writing his or her book. Compare your information with a partner and discuss why each of you arrived at your conclusions. Create a chart with advice you would give others on being a good listener.

PERFORMANCE TASK II:

QUALITY CRITERIA:
"LOOK FORS"

- Listen attentively and critically to the messages.
- Interpret the messages.
- Identify significant and insignificant information.
- Compare your information with information someone else gathered.
- Ask questions.
- Draw appropriate conclusions about listening.
- Develop a chart based on your conclusion.

You have been working on your listening skills. A doctor or some other community expert will be visiting your class to explain new advances in his or her field. To prepare for the presentation, write some questions you could ask to clarify points of interest. Listen carefully to the speaker. Take notes of the key points, and then ask your questions to gain more information. Following the presentation, write what you hear the speaker say about the topic. Compare your information with a partner, and discuss how you arrived at your conclusion. Create a chart explaining how questioning helps a listener gain information.

**Language Arts:
Grade 8**

**Performance
Benchmark**

LISTENING
CONTENT/CONCEPT STANDARDS 2, 3

KEY ORGANIZING QUESTION:

What can be learned by being a critical listener?

KEY COMPETENCES	KEY CONCEPTS AND CONTENT	PERFORMANCE TASKS
Listen Record Analyze Compare Contrast Design Model	Critical analysis of speakers' message and approach. Compare and contrast points of view.	**PERFORMANCE TASK I:** Your class is going to create a newscast as part of its study of major U.S. conflicts, past and present. To prepare for the newscast, your teacher plays a tape of three different TV newscasters. Listen to the newscasters; identify and describe the three approaches to delivering the news. Compare and contrast the differences in styles you noticed with the differences identified by your teammates. Develop your newscast using selected approaches you heard, and present it to your classmates. Ask them to discuss your delivery style. What caught their attention?

PERFORMANCE TASK II:

Your teacher plays a tape of a series of advertisements that are used on the Saturday morning cartoon shows. Identify and analyze the techniques that are used in the advertisements. Compare and contrast the techniques. Select a product you could advertise on the Saturday morning cartoon shows. Design and develop a commercial using selected techniques that you have identified, and present your commercial to your classmates. Ask them to respond to your commercial by identifying what they liked best about what they heard.

**QUALITY CRITERIA:
"LOOK FORS"**

- Listen attentively and critically to the messages and how they are delivered.
- Record significant information that defines distinctions.
- Identify organizational patterns and approaches of delivering information.
- Compare and contrast various delivery approaches.
- Create a script for a commercial.
- Model presentation after selected approaches.

Language Arts:
Grade 12

Performance
Benchmark

LISTENING
CONTENT/CONCEPT STANDARD 3

KEY ORGANIZING QUESTION:

What role does listening play at work and in sports?

KEY COMPETENCES	KEY CONCEPTS AND CONTENT	PERFORMANCE TASKS
Identify Interview Record Synthesize Analyze Organize Present Recommend	Collect information about: Listening skills in the workplace. Listening skills in sports.	**PERFORMANCE TASK I:** Many careers require keen listening abilities: Doctors listen to hearts and lungs; mechanics listen to the sound of an engine; psychologists listen to what patients say and don't say; priests listen to confessions; food servers listen to orders; and so on. Select several careers and interview people in those careers about the role listening plays in their daily work routines. Identify the listening activities essential to these careers. Synthesize and analyze your data and organize it for presentation to a 10th- or 11th-grade English class. Provide details and give examples of the role listening plays in these careers. Include recommendations for teachers that would help students better develop their listening skills.

QUALITY CRITERIA:
"LOOK FORS"

- Define your purpose.
- Prepare, clear, concise questions.
- Focus on the task.
- Record essential information.
- Synthesize and analyze findings.
- Select most appropriate information according to your purpose.
- Organize data according to your purpose.
- Present findings using standard conventions for audience.
- Recommend insights for improving listening skills.

PERFORMANCE TASK II:

Identify a sport you enjoy playing or watching. Identify the listening activities involved in playing the sport. Interview people who play and coach the sport. Prepare the presentation for your class on the "Importance of Listening" in this specific sport. Provide details and give examples of the role listening plays in the sport. Compare listening in this sport with listening in other sports. Explain how this sport might be affected if listening weren't present. Include recommendations that you think would help students develop their listening skills to a greater degree.

SPEAKING

Content/Concept Standards

Speaking and listening, the oral language arts skills, are used more frequently than reading and writing. As part of developing their skills as effective communicators, students draw upon the languages of their homes, their communities, their cultures, and the public languages of the larger culture. Student competence in these skills is critical to success in academic learning and participation in the life of the community. Although students have many speaking and listening experiences before they enter school, they still have much to learn to become confident, responsible, clear, adaptive, and fluent communicators. Their growing competence also includes participation in technological formats such as radio, television, and computer networks.

Instructional Issues in Speaking

Since speaking is something that students do before they come to school, the school can build on the skills already developed, keeping in mind that acquisition and development of all languages follows predictable patterns. To continue to develop their speaking ability, students need numerous opportunities to communicate in a variety of situations. They need to engage in discussions and conversations to clarify their thoughts; explore issues, feelings, and experiences; and extend their understanding. School must be filled with students' talk.

Speaking Strategies

The emphasis in teaching speaking is on the dynamic process of oral communication, the structure of communication, the delivery of communication, and the feedback from a communication experience. Communication capabilities will become more complex as students move through the developmental stages.

What all speakers should know and be able to do

Develop the content for a message:

- Analyze the audience
- Consider various elements of evidence and reasoning
- Frame the ideas in appropriate language

Organize the structure of the message:

- Develop a clear central idea
- Identify the various purposes of communication
- Develop an introduction, body, conclusion

Make the presentation:

- Select and use the appropriate presentation style to fit the communication situation: conversation, storytelling, discussion, reporting, giving directions, explaining, dramatization, dramatics, reading aloud, and debate
- Speak in a style that is effective for specific communication experiences
- Select and use vocal strategies to produce effective and intentional meanings
- Use appropriate language
- Apply nonverbal characteristics (eye contact, facial expression, posture, gestures, movement, and personal appearance) in diverse communication experiences
- Incorporate the use of audiovisual aids that adapt to the audience, situation, and environment

Seek feedback:

- Adjust messages and speaking techniques to conditions preceding, during, or following the message
- Ask questions of audience members to involve others in the communication process
- Encourage audience participation in response to presentation
- Analyze and evaluate self and others' oral presentations and discussions

The strategies for speaking are integral to the following performance benchmarks for each grade level.

What students should know how to do by the end of Grade 3

Students continue to build upon the language skills that have been developed within their homes and community. They increase their speaking skills through conversations, group communications, and oral presentations and develop a vocabulary that enables them to describe, reason, explain, and use qualitative words. They discuss topics and issues that are significant to them and become more confident in a variety of situations and with a range of audiences. To strengthen their speaking skills and their confidence, students need a risk-free environment with many opportunities for oral communications: role-playing, choral reading, debates, oral reports, discussions, creative dramatics, interviewing, demonstrations, radio and TV production. They should be able to

1. Retell stories from listening, writing, reading, and looking at pictures
2. Participate in collaborative speaking activities such as choral reading, plays, skits, and reciting poems
3. Contribute to class and small group discussions
4. Explore and solve problems with others
5. Dramatize a story or an event
6. Express thoughts and feelings in complete sentences
7. Introduce people and respond to introductions
8. Speak before a group to express an opinion, present information, or tell a story
9. Telephone others for social calls
10. Give directions
11. Investigate social problems that exist in their communities, society, environment, and the world using oral language as a tool

What students should know how to do by the end of Grade 5

Students demonstrate increased competence in speaking for a variety of purposes in a variety of contexts for authentic audiences. They improve their oral communication skills by talking and listening across the curriculum. They solve problems in social studies through small group discussions and projects; they report orally on the results of science experiments; they dramatize stories from literature; they express their thoughts and feelings during writing conferences; they read literature aloud; and they talk through math problems with others. Through oral communications, students explore the world around them, appreciate the diverse culture of others, and develop their interpersonal skills. They should be able to

1. Report orally on a project using a cause-and-effect pattern
2. Initiate and build on ideas in a brainstorming session
3. Role-play a character from literature or an event
4. Question another person when seeking further information about a topic
5. Present a persuasive talk to the class about a school or community project

6. Interview members of the school and community

7. Summarize the main ideas of a report (e.g., history, science, social studies) given by a classmate

8. Participate in a small-group discussion in class

9. Present components of a simple process

10. Participate in mock telephone conversations on diverse topics for a variety of purposes

11. Discuss concepts in one content area and relate them to another content area

12. Engage in dialogue and debate concerning important community, state, national, and international events

What students should know how to do by the end of Grade 8

Students increase their ability to interact more effectively with their peers and with adults. They express themselves well in a variety of situations and on a range of topics, articulating their ideas, thoughts, and feelings with confidence and clarity. They apply positive interpersonal and social skills in their daily interaction by listening to others and showing respect for diverse beliefs. Opportunities for dramatic expression and creative drama provide students with motivation for using language effectively in a variety of situations. They should be able to

1. Present an oral interpretation of a literary selection

2. Ask questions to clarify texts, situations, and issues

3. Improvise a series of situations

4. Design and produce commercials and newscasts

5. Summarize and paraphrase ideas presented by others

6. Participate in small- and large-group discussions by asking and responding to questions and by identifying and solving problems

7. Demonstrate how to do something or how to make something

8. Participate in panel discussions, presentations, informal debates, and dramatic interpretations

9. Articulate generalizations and apply concepts and new vocabulary across content areas

10. Engage in critical study, reflection, and analysis of social, ethical, and moral problems and dilemmas that arise in historical and contemporary fiction and nonfiction

11. Engage in dialogue and debate concerning important community, state, national, and international events

What students should know how to do by the end of Grade 12

Students demonstrate the ability to engage constructively in the exchange of ideas during class discussions. They use creativity and critical thinking to identify and solve problems by participating in a variety of group decision-making and problem-solving activities. They access information and apply knowledge by researching topics for their speeches, taking notes, organizing their ideas, and writing outlines. They develop awareness and perception of levels of language and extended meanings. They participate in many of the following speech activities using many forms of literature, electronic media, and music: public speaking, debates, panel discussions, class meetings, interviewing, announcing, simulated broadcasting, impromptu speaking, improvisations. They should be able to

1. Develop and defend arguments in a variety of situations

2. Role-play a variety of situations and events

3. Deliver informal or impromptu speeches on a variety of topics

4. Deliver persuasive and other formal speeches

5. Participate in formal debates

6. Engage in parliamentary procedure
7. Conduct a large-group meeting
8. Participate in dramatic interpretations
9. Engage in critical study, reflection, and analysis of social, ethical, and moral problems and dilemmas that arise in historical and contemporary fiction and nonfiction
10. Dialogue, debate, and respond to community, state, national, and international events
11. Engage in long-term community or action research projects and community service projects for which they will use language effectively to study, document, and present the project chosen

Language Arts:
Grade 3

Performance
Benchmark

SPEAKING
CONTENT/CONCEPT STANDARDS 2, 5, 8

KEY ORGANIZING QUESTION:

How can you use a skit to convey an important message?

KEY COMPETENCES	KEY CONCEPTS AND CONTENT	PERFORMANCE TASKS
Identify Collect Collaborate Practice Present	Plan and perform a verbal and visual message.	**PERFORMANCE TASK I:** As a team, collect the necessary information on your topic (e.g., "Say No to Drugs"). Review all of the information and select the important ideas you want your audience to learn. Develop the script for your skit. Design necessary props and create simple costumes. Practice your skit. Present it to a group of classmates and get feedback from them. How could you make it better? Make necessary changes. Arrange to present your skit to another class. Ask them to make a poster showing the message in your skit.

QUALITY CRITERIA:
"LOOK FORS"

- Identify major purpose and topic of the skit.
- Collect essential content and materials for presentation.
- Collaborate effectively with others in planning and practicing skit.
- Arrange for presentation with another class.
- Present information in a meaningful and interesting manner.
- Request pictures or posters from your audience.

PERFORMANCE TASK II:
You must design a skit for kindergarten students that will convince them to eat healthy snacks. Review necessary information about food groups and healthy snacks. Select your key ideas and develop a simple skit. Rehearse your skit and get feedback from a group of classmates. Make necessary changes and rehearse again. Arrange to present your skit to the kindergarten class. Ask the kindergartners to draw a picture showing your message about healthy snacks.

SPEAKING
CONTENT/CONCEPT STANDARDS 5, 6

KEY ORGANIZING QUESTION:

Can you persuade others to accept your conclusions about an issue?

KEY COMPETENCES	KEY CONCEPTS AND CONTENT	PERFORMANCE TASKS
Interview Discuss Summarize Persuade	Prepare for and conduct an interview. Present a persuasive speech.	**PERFORMANCE TASK I:** Design and develop a survey form you can use in collecting data from your class-mates on the amount of time they watch TV in 1 week and the amount of time they engage in physical exercise in 1 week. Ask questions to collect your data. Summarize the data and review. Discuss the findings and take a stand. Plan a persuasive speech to get others to accept your position. Use charts and illustrations to support your stand. Ask students to cast a secret ballot after your presentation on whether they agree with your position. **PERFORMANCE TASK II:** Design and develop a survey form to collect information on the kinds of foods students in your class have for snacks. Ask questions and collect your data. Summarize the data and review. Discuss the findings. Take a stand. Plan a persuasive speech to get others to accept your position. Use charts and illustrations to support your stand. After your presentation, have students cast a secret ballot on whether they agree with your position.

QUALITY CRITERIA:
"LOOK FORS"

• Prepare a survey form for use in your interview.
• Conduct interview using key questions.
• Carefully record the collected data.
• Summarize the collected data.
• Develop your position.
• Design a convincing presentation.
• Review the results.

Language Arts:
Grade 8

SPEAKING
CONTENT/CONCEPT STANDARD 8

KEY ORGANIZING QUESTION:

What questions about a career are most important, and how can people learn about a particular career?

KEY COMPETENCES	KEY CONCEPTS AND CONTENT	PERFORMANCE TASKS
Identify Gather Organize Present Respond	Panel discussion. Class discussion.	**PERFORMANCE TASK I:** Your class has decided to provide career information for other students. Divide students into teams. Each member of the team will identify a career he or she will research. After each member of your team has gathered the information about the career he or she has chosen, design and develop a panel discussion for another class emphasizing the benefits of specific careers. In addition to making your panel presentation, you have to respond to questions from the audience. Identify the kinds of questions you might be asked and plan appropriate responses. After the panel presentation, ask students to respond to a survey on their top choices for a career.

QUALITY CRITERIA:
"LOOK FORS"

- Identify topic for presentation.
- Gather relevant information from a variety of resources.
- Organize material for effective presentation.
- Present information using effective techniques.
- Respond appropriately to audience feedback.

PERFORMANCE TASK II:

Identify a career to research. Gather as much meaningful information as you can so you can be considered an "expert" on a specific career. Prepare a commercial (audio, video, or both) for recruiting others to the career you have chosen. "Broadcast" your commercial to other members of your class or other students in your school. Have students respond on a numbered continuum from 1 to 5 indicating the degree to which your commercial affected their level of interest in your career.

Language Arts:
Grade 12

Performance
Benchmark

SPEAKING
CONTENT/CONCEPT STANDARDS 1, 4, 5

KEY ORGANIZING QUESTION:

What speaking techniques are most effective to persuade others concerning social and political issues?

KEY COMPETENCES	KEY CONCEPTS AND CONTENT	PERFORMANCE TASKS
Identify Select Organize Analyze Synthesize Debate Persuade Respond Question	Debate. Persuasive speech.	**PERFORMANCE TASK I:** Contemporary music often addresses political and social issues about which people disagree. In teams, listen to some examples of contemporary songs that deal with such issues. Identify those issues that cause disagreement. Select one of the issues for a debate and determine positions that you and your teammates will argue for the debate. Stage the debate for the other students in your class, attempting to persuade them to accept your position. Respond to questions and ask questions of others as appropriate. Provide a survey for your audience members where they can record their opinion of your persuasiveness at the end of the debate. **PERFORMANCE TASK II:**

QUALITY CRITERIA:
"LOOK FORS"

- Identify major political and social issues in various text.
- Identify precisely areas of disagreement among individuals.
- Select an issue and determine a position to debate.
- Analyze and synthesize information for the debate.
- Participate fully in the debate.
- Respond appropriately to questions.
- Generate effective questions for a survey.

Brainstorm and create a list of political and social issues that are dealt with in various works of literature. Identify issues about which there are differences of opinion by different authors. Select one of the issues and prepare a debate with another student in which each of you defend a different author's viewpoint. Respond to questions of others as appropriate. Provide a survey for your audience where they can record their opinion of your presentation at the end of the debate.

WRITING

Content/Concept Standards

Writing is a powerful tool for thinking and learning as well as a process for communicating. Writing helps us generate, develop, organize, modify, critique, and remember our ideas. By writing, we crystallize and scrutinize our thoughts and feelings in a way that is seldom possible through speech. Writing provides visual proof of our thoughts, feelings, and ideas; writing is "seeing our thinking" on paper.

Writing is a difficult and complex skill. It is the skill most widely required by students as a demonstration of their learning. At the same time, it is one of the most difficult to master because it requires thinking about and doing many different things at once. It is the process of selecting, developing, and arranging ideas effectively. Writing requires students to use a variety of forms, for a variety of purposes, and for a variety of audiences. Each form, purpose, and audience demands different styles, approaches, and word choices.

Instructional Issues in Writing

Writing includes composing with words, illustrations, video, and other technological and symbolic forms. As students develop as writers, they gain increasing control over the variety of ways in which human cultures represent information, ideas, and experiences. These representations include text, drawings, graphs, diagrams, photographs, videos, and computer graphics.

Students who learn to write using a process of **prewriting**, **drafting**, **revising**, **proofreading**, and **publishing** in stages perform better than students taught any other way. During the process, students as writers move back and forth recursively from one stage of writing to another, reflecting the real-world way in which writers produce writing.

Writers must learn the mechanics of writing: spelling, grammar, usage, punctuation, capitalization, and format. When and how students learn these conventions is all-important. Students must learn them in a writing context; they must apply them during the revision stage of writing; and they must receive focused, direct instruction based on their individual writing needs.

Writing Strategies

The emphasis in teaching writing strategies is on the recursive process in which writers produce written products. Each of the recursive stages involved in writing contains many skills. Students must have a command of these skills and be able to apply them as necessary when they are engaged as writers.

What all writers should know and be able to do

Prewrite: Generate and discover ideas

• Read	• Draw	• Speak	• Experience
• Listen	• Dramatize	• Brainstorm	• Sense intuitively
• Interview	• Recall	• Research	• Empathize
• Classify	• Imagine	• Visualize	• Dream

Draft: Discover, organize and record thoughts

- Choose a topic
- Invent spellings to record ideas
- Record experiences, feelings, and ideas
- Restart
- Add or delete ideas
- Create images
- Connect ideas
- Consider audience and format
- Adjust style to the genre, subject, purpose, and audience
- Share with others
- Continue reading and researching

Revise: Reorganize and develop the subject matter to better suit the audience and purpose

- Add and delete information
- Seek help
- Refine purpose
- Share with peers
- Consider arrangement of sentences, paragraphs, and images
- Select precise language
- Use a dictionary and thesaurus
- Evaluate
- Predict audience reaction

Proofread: Attend to punctuation, spelling, word choice, usage, and form

- Correct sentence fragments and run-on sentences when appropriate
- Correct sentence syntax errors
- Correct errors in usage, such as lack of subject-verb agreement and incorrect verb tense
- Correct punctuation and capitalization
- Correct illegible handwriting
- Correct format problems
- Identify and correct misspelled and misused words

Publish: Prepare selected pieces for publication

- Prepare corrected copy for publication
- Share the piece with appropriate audiences
- Enjoy the published works of classmates

The strategies in the five stages of writing — **prewriting**, **drafting**, **revising**, **proofreading**, and **publishing** — are integral to the performance benchmarks that follow for each grade level.

What students should know how to do by the end of Grade 3

At this level, students enjoy their own ideas and have the confidence to share what they are thinking. Through their writing, students express much about life and about themselves. They need a wide variety of real and vicarious experiences and many opportunities for writing about topics that are relevant and have meaning, importance, and significance for them. Essential to their growth in writing is their need to read widely and experience all forms of expression: drama, music, art, and movement. As they mature as writers, they use a variety of sentence structures, both simple and complex, complete and incomplete. They develop an awareness of audience by including more details and background information. They expand their use of adjectives and adverbs, and they learn to spell the words they need. They want and are ready for a variety of spelling strategies and resources. They use capitals, question marks, periods, possessives, and contractions correctly. They revise when they are encouraged to do so by peers or the teacher. They make special efforts in revision and proofreading in order to publish their work for the class, school, and community. Because they are frequently discouraged by the magnitude of this task, they need help, encouragement, and recognition. They keep examples of their work in various stages of the writing process in their portfolios and use them as a means of conferencing, assessing, and reporting to their parents. They should be able to

1. Contribute to small-group and entire-class stories, poems, songs, and plays
2. Create stories, letters, poems, messages, invitations, advertisements, reports, plays, directions, interviews, instructions, and agendas
3. Write a paragraph about an issue of concern using a topic sentence and supporting details
4. Keep a journal
5. Write for different audiences including the teacher, peers, family, and the principal
6. Write a short report using one or two references
7. Use publishing strategies such as self-correction and legible writing to clarify meaning

What students should know how to do by the end of Grade 5

Students' writing skills continue to develop as they write, revise, and publish texts that are diverse in content and form for a variety of purposes and audiences. They increase their ability to take notes from various sources of information, abstracting main ideas and facts relevant to the subject and purpose of a report. They discover and use writing as an effective tool for learning in other content areas where they write and think critically about a variety of issues, concepts, ideas, and topics. They grow in their ability to use vocabulary that is vivid and precise. Working with peer groups and conferencing with the teacher, they revise and edit their work for appropriate spelling, usage, and mechanics and become constructive and critical members of a community of writers. When students are engaged in meaningful writing activities, they are also developing skills that are necessary for effective reading. They should be able to

1. Use illustration and classification to develop a theme
2. Develop a personal story, expository piece, or position paper, and write several related paragraphs
3. Sequence written materials as part of a report or presentation
4. Organize details or events in a logical sequence
5. Construct an opinion about an argument or discussion
6. Prepare a bibliography and appropriate documentation for a report or demonstration
7. Use publishing strategies such as self-correction and legible writing to clarify meaning
8. Use writing as a means of self-expression and self-understanding, as a way of learning, and as a vehicle for meaningful communication with others

What students should know how to do by the end of Grade 8

Students expand their skills and techniques in both functional and creative writing. They write for others on a variety of levels and for a variety of purposes, using such forms as history reports, science projects, essay answers, research papers, and letters. They must state an idea clearly and support it, they must organize and develop an argument in a systematic way, and they must be increasingly impersonal and objective as the situation becomes more formal. For creative writing, they must reduce the distance between themselves and their audience, use imaginative words rather than clichés, and open their writing to more subjective interpretation. At this level, students are capable of demonstrating considerable ability in correcting spelling, punctuation, and usage, and in improving drafts of their writing. They must write with clarity, order, economy, and vividness, using figurative and precise language. They should be able to

1. Write several related paragraphs around a theme leading to a conclusion, using appropriate transitions
2. Develop a composition using definition, analysis, and comparison and contrast
3. Support generalizations with relevant facts and data
4. Expand meaning using figurative language (simile, metaphor) and analogies
5. Clarify meaning using publishing strategies such as self-correction and legible writing
6. Incorporate a wide variety of forms and genres, for example, narration, description, exposition, and poetry
7. Write a research paper using several sources to document information
8. Identify and use the different purposes, audiences, and contexts for writing, and identify and use appropriately different types of vocabulary, tones, levels of language, stylistic devices, types of sentence structure, and images

What students should know how to do by the end of Grade 12

Students develop their individual styles and are able to write for a variety of purposes and audiences. They use writing as a powerful tool for sharing information and knowledge, for influencing and persuading, and for creating and entertaining. Students write with considerable fluency and ease, and continuing refinement should be evident in their work. They must manipulate structure and vocabulary to affect tone and style, and they must support opinions and judgments with authoritative information. They must gather information from primary and secondary sources; write a report using this research; quote, paraphrase, and summarize accurately; and cite sources properly. Students must respond to literature with a variety of writings including analysis, personal responses, and poems. Through writing and writing-to-learn strategies, they reflect and explore their ideas and feelings; they increase knowledge and meaning; they communicate ideas; and they validate their learning. They should be able to

1. Develop a thesis statement and expand it into an essay
2. Develop multiparagraph reports and assignments using a variety of forms: expository, descriptive, narrative, and persuasive
3. Complete various forms: tax returns, applications, and questionnaires
4. Create a résumé
5. Write a research paper that includes an introductory statement, relevant facts on the topic, logical presentation, conclusions, and bibliography
6. Analyze the different perspectives taken by authors in a variety of genres
7. Clarify meaning using publishing strategies such as self-correction and legible writing
8. Dialogue, debate, and respond to (in the form of editorials, bulletins, newspaper reporting, etc.) community, state, national, and international events
9. Use information sources to construct research on a culture or groups of people from a specific point of view

Language Arts:
Grade 3

WRITING
CONTENT/CONCEPT STANDARDS 2, 5

KEY ORGANIZING QUESTION:

What makes a story interesting?

KEY COMPETENCES	KEY CONCEPTS AND CONTENT	PERFORMANCE TASKS
Design	Write a story using material obtained from personal interviews.	**PERFORMANCE TASK I:** Just about everyone has a best friend. Design and develop a series of questions about best friends and use them to conduct an interview with a classmate on the subject of "best friends." Record the pertinent information. Write a story about best friends for the class newspaper based on your interview with your classmate.
Develop		
Interview		
Record		
Organize		
Draft		
Revise		
Proofread		
Publish		**PERFORMANCE TASK II:**

QUALITY CRITERIA:
"LOOK FORS"

- Design and develop appropriate questions for an interview.
- Interview necessary person(s).
- Record accurate notes.
- Organize notes.
- Develop story with supporting details.
- Revise words and sentences for clarifying meaning.
- Share with a fellow student for feedback and recommendations and revise.
- Proofread for punctuation, capitalization, and spelling.
- Submit for publication.

PERFORMANCE TASK II:
Design and develop a series of questions that you can ask an adult about his or her most exciting memories of childhood. Conduct your interview and write a story from your notes. You will read your story to another class, and it will be put into a class book that eventually will be placed in the school media center.

Language Arts:
Grade 5

Performance
Benchmark

WRITING
CONTENT/CONCEPT STANDARD 4

KEY ORGANIZING QUESTION:

How do you write the necessary instructions to explain something that someone has never done before?

KEY COMPETENCES	KEY CONCEPTS AND CONTENT	PERFORMANCE TASKS
Select Organize Draft Revise Proofread	Write detailed and accurate instructions.	**PERFORMANCE TASK I:** Games are universal and enjoyed by young and old. Select one game that you and members of your family play and write the instructions for that game. Have the students in your class play the game using your written instructions. Ask students to give you feedback on the accuracy of your instructions, and revise them until they work for a group that hasn't played the game.

QUALITY CRITERIA:
"LOOK FORS"

- Select appropriate information.
- Draft specific, clear, detailed, and accurate instructions.
- Test instructions for clarity and accuracy.
- Revise language and sentence order.
- Proofread punctuation, capitalization, and spelling.
- Use the instructions to achieve the purpose.

PERFORMANCE TASK II:

A guest speaker from the zoo is coming to talk to your class. The speaker has never been to your classroom before. Write clear and accurate directions that will get the speaker from the front door of your school to your classroom or your meeting place using the most direct route. To check your instructions, have several classmates test them and give you feedback on the results.

Language Arts:
Grade 8

Performance
Benchmark

WRITING
CONTENT/CONCEPT STANDARD 4

KEY ORGANIZING QUESTION:

What role does figurative language play in song lyrics and poetry?

KEY COMPETENCES	KEY CONCEPTS AND CONTENT	PERFORMANCE TASKS
Generate Organize Record Extend Revise Proofread Publish	Write and analyze poetry using figurative language and analogies.	**PERFORMANCE TASK I:** Your teacher has announced that the middle schools in your district will produce an anthology of student poetry that will be submitted to a national contest. All middle school students are invited to submit their original poetry to a team of editors composed of students from all of the schools. You decide to write and submit a poem that will contain figurative language and analogies. Write your poem and share it with several students for their reaction. Make the appropriate revisions from their feedback before submitting your poem for publication.

PERFORMANCE TASK II:

List three of your favorite songs. Identify examples of figurative language used in the lyrics. Write an article for the school newspaper explaining how and why the songwriters used that figurative language in writing their song lyrics. Present your article to your classmates and have them respond to your article. Make the appropriate revisions before submitting your article for publication.

QUALITY CRITERIA:
"LOOK FORS"

- Generate ideas for writing.
- Organize and record thoughts.
- Use effective figurative language and analogies to extend meaning.
- Proofread writing for accurate punctuation, spelling, word choice, usage, and form.
- Prepare the selected piece for publication.

Language Arts:
Grade 12

Performance
Benchmark

WRITING
CONTENT/CONCEPT STANDARDS 2, 4

KEY ORGANIZING QUESTION:
How can a résumé be designed to best convey information about you to a potential employer?

KEY COMPETENCES	KEY CONCEPTS AND CONTENT	PERFORMANCE TASKS
Identify Draft Revise Proofread Submit	Complete an application form. Write a résumé.	**PERFORMANCE TASK I:** Your school is having a Career Expo during which a variety of employers will be present to describe their companies and the types of jobs that are available for summer as well as year-round. Select a company that might participate in the Expo and identify a summer job you want to get at that company. Write a résumé and complete the company's application form to use in applying for the summer job. **PERFORMANCE TASK II:** Many students in your class are seeking summer jobs that require them to submit an application and a résumé. You offer a service that includes completing job applications and writing résumés. A customer who wants to apply for a job with the parks and recreation department asks for your services. Design and develop a résumé for that customer and provide assistance in completing the application. Or select a career field other students are interested in. Research the kinds of skills needed in that field and prepare a sample résumé addressing those skills. Ask a person from a personnel department in that field to critique your sample résumé. Offer your services in writing résumés and applications to other students in your school who wish to apply in that field.

QUALITY CRITERIA:
"LOOK FORS"
• Identify and access key information.
• Draft a résumé.
• Complete an application accurately.
• Revise the résumé to better suit the audience and purpose.
• Proofread the résumé and application for accurate punctuation, spelling, word choice, usage, and form.
• Submit the résumé and application to appropriate audience.

READING

Content/Concept Standards

Readers construct meaning by interacting with visual materials on the basis of their existing or prior knowledge about the world. Readers react to the visual materials and combine previous knowledge and information with the new information they read in the visual materials. It is this combining of new information with old that we call "constructing meaning." The more students read, write, view, speak, and listen, and the more experiences they have, the more their prior knowledge grows, which in turn strengthens their ability to construct meaning.

Instructional Issues in Reading

Reading is the process of constructing meaning through the dynamic interaction among the reader's existing knowledge, the information suggested by the written language, and the context of the situation. Reading, or constructing meaning from visual materials, is not simply getting most of the words right. It includes making sense of literature, exposition, media, and other texts including print materials, film, television, and other technological and symbolic displays. As they advance in grade level, students must develop increasingly sophisticated and complex skills in understanding, appreciating, and evaluating what they read. They must apply a bank of strategies in increasingly complex situations that enable them to negotiate an ever-growing array of genres, purposes, and text formats. Through these texts, students are immersed in great traditions and profit from the best the various cultures in our society have to offer. They encounter the minds of great writers and thinkers and deal with universal concerns of every age and society. Students make authentic connections to the world outside the classroom and validate their responses through class discussions, simulations, cooperative learning, writing, and visual projects and presentations.

Readers must be able to recognize words quickly and accurately in order to construct the meaning of the text. Phonemic awareness, which involves an ability to hear the sounds in a word and to distinguish between words based on the different sounds, is an important predictor of success in learning to read. Phonics instruction, teaching the relationship between letters and sounds, can help children attain automatic, visual recognition of spelling patterns within words for word recognition. Three cueing systems that readers use to gain meaning from texts are semantics (meaning), syntax (context), and phonics. Good readers ask themselves these questions:

> Does it make sense? (semantics)
> Does it sound right? (syntax)
> Do the sounds match the symbols? (phonics)

Effective beginning reading instruction contains a balance of activities designed to improve word recognition, including phonics instruction and reading meaningful text. Phonics instruction is most effective when it is done in relationship to connected, informative, engaging text.

Reading for meaning should be paramount in the reading process. The simultaneous use of the three cueing systems facilitates this process.

Reading Strategies

Effective readers use strategies to construct meaning **before**, **during**, and **after** reading. As students master these strategies, they become independent learners who read with confidence and enjoyment. Reading becomes a dynamic process for interacting with an author's thoughts, a tool for learning, and a source of personal fulfillment.

What all readers should know and be able to do

Before reading:

- Establish the purpose for reading and predict the type of text
- Generate questions
- Make predictions from the title and pictures of what the text will be about
- Activate prior knowledge and experiences

During reading:

- Generate questions
- Strategically decode (context clues, phonics, semantics)
- Monitor for meaning and word order and self-correct when something does not make sense
- Confirm and revise predictions
- Adjust rate to accommodate purpose, style, and difficulty of text
- Formulate vocabulary meaning, concepts, themes, major ideas, and supporting ideas from within and across texts
- Make inferences and draw conclusions
- Identify specific information
- Evaluate and react critically to text
- Apply concepts to other experiences

After reading:

- Summarize important information
- Generate questions
- Evaluate and react critically to text
- Analyze and reflect upon personal reading performance
- Apply concepts to other experiences

The **before**, **during**, and **after** reading strategies are integral to the following performance benchmarks for each grade level.

What students should know how to do by the end of Grade 3

Students use reading to satisfy their curiosity, to gain information, and as a source of personal enjoyment and enrichment. They read a variety of materials including poetry, fantasy, folk literature, animal stories, biographies, reference books, textbooks, newspapers, and magazines. They continue to develop their ability to bring meaning to and to get meaning from print using all the cueing systems. They expect to make sense of reading using text features and experiences to make predictions. As they read, they use prior knowledge, monitor their understanding, and use appropriate strategies to make sense of what they read. Through various classroom activities and approaches in which reading, writing, listening, and speaking are integrated, students experience growth in their ability to read fluently and critically. They should be able to

1. Select and use appropriate sections of a book for finding information for a report presentation or project: index, table of contents, glossary, and bibliography

2. Gather information from a variety of texts, including media and graphic sources such as pictures, cartoons, diagrams, charts, maps, and tables

3. Acquire information and enrich personal vocabulary by reading

4. Act in personally, socially, and civically responsible ways using the knowledge gained from text

5. Compare and contrast experiences reflected in culturally diverse texts with student's own culture and the cultures of others

6. Explain the main idea and details in a text

7. Identify causes and effects based on information within a text

8. Evaluate and generate statements of opinion and personal preference

9. Assess the value of information

10. Predict, confirm, and self-correct to construct, examine, and extend meaning in various texts

11. Select materials appropriate to their identified purposes for reading

12. Construct, examine, and extend meaning for novels and other more complex multicultural literature

13. Research and learn about one's own and other cultures using multiple reference materials

14. Read fluently with expression and self-correction

15. Read appropriate literature and materials (applies to children learning English as a second language)

16. Predict what will happen next in the story based on story meanings, illustrations, and word meanings

17. Read a variety of literature

What students should know how to do by the end of Grade 5

At this level, students read from a variety of sources for their own interest and to broaden understanding of themselves and others. They understand increasingly difficult material and are able to read more critically and analytically. They make predictions with greater accuracy and increase their ability to generalize what they learn from a text to new or different situations. They increase their ability to gain knowledge and ideas from multiple resources, including multimedia. Through literature, they interact with and appreciate people from diverse cultures, and they learn about human conditions that occur across time and space. Students read literature and texts as models for improving in their own writing. In order to become more skillful, reflective, and confident readers, students must be actively engaged in generating questions, interacting with others, writing responses to texts, thinking critically, and monitoring their understanding. They should be able to

1. Locate and use human, print, and electronic information and resources from multiple sources

2. Detect bias, prejudice, stereotyping, and propaganda in text and understand their negative effects on individuals

3. Explain the elements of character, setting, plot, theme, and resolution in a fictional work

4. Identify the structure of nonfiction: major ideas and supporting details

5. Identify and appreciate a variety of genres from diverse cultures and authors

6. Analyze the cause-and-effect relationships in a text

7. Compare and contrast information from different sources

8. Generalize what was learned from the text to different or new situations

9. Illustrate an appreciation for diversity through text

10. Predict, confirm, and self-correct to construct, examine, and extend meaning in various texts

11. Reflect on and share interpretations of a text through discussion

12. Read a range of literature that is rich in quality and is representative of different cultures, literary forms, and historical periods

What students should know how to do by the end of Grade 8

Through reading and literature-related activities, students think about experiences, ideas, and feelings with increased clarity, logic, and sensitivity. They acquire interests and attitudes of maturing readers through reading and discussing a variety of literature, independent reading, listening and viewing multimedia, responding in writing, and oral reading. They also learn about and appreciate the diverse literary heritage that exists throughout the world. They are able to read a variety of materials with fluency and efficiency, and they know that the texts they read are potential models for their own work. Reading instruction at this level should challenge students to move from the concrete and known to the abstract and unknown. They should be able to

1. Identify different purposes of texts: persuasion, information, and narrative written by traditional and contemporary authors who represent a range of cultural traditions and backgrounds
2. Evaluate the validity, impact, and quality of texts
3. Broaden experiences through text
4. Apply relevant information from literature to real life experiences and to other literature
5. Explain author's techniques and purposes for point of view and figurative language
6. Identify organizational structures and purpose of informational text: enumeration, sequence, cause and effect, comparison and contrast, problem-solution
7. Analyze theme, tone, and style from a variety of genres
8. Illustrate an appreciation for diversity using text
9. Adjust reading rate and style (skimming, scanning, careful reading) to the purpose for reading
10. Detect bias, prejudice, and stereotyping in a variety of texts; recognize and understand their negative impacts on others; and counteract these efforts in their behaviors and attitude
11. Read literature to learn about human experiences
12. Read and construct a personal response to different viewpoints

What students should know how to do by the end of Grade 12

Students are capable of enjoying and reading with ease a wide range of materials at a mature reading level. Students have developed personal reading tastes and search out materials that are stimulating and challenging. They understand subtleties of humor and complexities of symbolism. Through reading, they probe philosophical issues that concern humans, such as the nature of justice and human discontent, and the ideals of love and peace. They can manipulate abstract concepts comfortably and independently and use their own knowledge and experience, as well as the ideas of other readers and writers, as a basis for evaluating the validity, impact, and quality of texts and the skill of authors. They should be able to

1. Compare and contrast the author's apparent intent and the reader's interpretation in texts that are representative of different cultures, time periods, and literary forms
2. Critique and compare texts using appropriate criteria
3. Identify the characteristics, purposes, and effectiveness of an author's style
4. Compare treatments of similar themes in different genres
5. Analyze interrelationships among concepts and themes
6. Illustrate an appreciation for diversity through the use of texts
7. Assess the value of information

Language Arts:
Grade 3

Performance
Benchmark

READING
CONTENT/CONCEPT STANDARDS 1, 2, 4

KEY ORGANIZING QUESTION:

How do we find information to increase our knowledge and understanding of the past?

KEY COMPETENCES	KEY CONCEPTS AND CONTENT	PERFORMANCE TASKS
Locate Select Write Collect Discuss Create Present Evaluate	Read to find information. Access information from a variety of sources. Collect and combine materials. Create a product.	**PERFORMANCE TASK I:** Your school will soon celebrate its 50th anniversary, and the principal has asked all classes to participate in a special presentation. Your class has divided up into teams, and your team has decided to put together a book about what was happening in your community 50 years ago. Use your media center, family members, and community to find and gather ideas, materials, and information for your book. As your team finds materials, share and organize them into a book that you will publish and present to the school. **PERFORMANCE TASK II:** Your town will be celebrating its centennial. The city council is inviting students in the town to submit a scrapbook describing what was happening in the community and around the country 100 years ago. You decide to make and submit a scrapbook. Use your media center and your public library to locate and read materials and information that will make your scrapbook interesting and informative to people who live in your community. Organize the materials you collect, then design and publish your scrapbook.

QUALITY CRITERIA:
"LOOK FORS"

• Locate relevant information from a variety of sources.
• Select and use appropriate materials.
• Write complete notes on events and people.
• Collect appropriate graphic materials.
• Discuss and share information with team members.
• Create a product that accurately depicts the time period.
• Present the product to selected audience.
• Evaluate the product using self- and peer-evaluation checklists.

Language Arts: Grade 5

READING
CONTENT/CONCEPT STANDARDS 1, 5, 7, 9, 12

KEY ORGANIZING QUESTION:
How do I understand people who are different from me?

KEY COMPETENCES	KEY CONCEPTS AND CONTENT	PERFORMANCE TASKS
Locate Read Identify Compile Perform	Diversity: Appreciation and understanding of diverse cultures through a variety of genres.	**PERFORMANCE TASK I:** To help new students adjust to this country and to help you learn about the cultures of others, your class will create a magazine in which you compare cultural similarities and differences between this country and another country. In preparation for the publishing of the magazine, select one country. Gather as much information as you can on this country. Compile your information. How are the two countries similar? How are they different? Prepare a chart comparing the similarities and differences. Present possible explanations for the similarities and differences to your class, and predict how you might feel if you were moving to this other country. How would you have to adjust? **PERFORMANCE TASK II:** Most Native American tribes were in this country long before Europeans and others settled here. Select a Native American tribe that lived in your area. Read factual information from two different sources that describes how the tribe lived. Prepare an oral report for your class emphasizing the similarities and differences between the traditions and lifestyles of that tribe and your traditions and lifestyles. Explain how you might feel if you had to live with this tribe. How would you have to adjust?

QUALITY CRITERIA:
"LOOK FORS"
• Locate appropriate and varied materials.
• Read a wide variety of materials.
• Identify cultural similarities and differences.
• Compile appropriate written and visual information.
• Present a clear and logical explanation.

Language Arts:
Grade 8

Performance
Benchmark

READING
CONTENT/CONCEPT STANDARDS 1, 2, 5

KEY ORGANIZING QUESTION:

Should we believe everything we read and see?

KEY COMPETENCES	KEY CONCEPTS AND CONTENT	PERFORMANCE TASKS
Read Identify Analyze Evaluate Compile Present	Identify persuasive texts and strategies. Identify author's techniques in using language.	**PERFORMANCE TASK I:** You have joined a committee on consumer awareness. Your task on this committee is to alert future consumers to the suggestive and persuasive language advertisers use to address potential customers. Read through various advertisements and commercials; compile examples of language manipulation to present to your class along with a list of techniques that consumers should be aware of when reading advertisements. Include recommendations for consumers that will aid their decision-making process.

QUALITY CRITERIA:
"LOOK FORS"

- Read a wide variety of advertisements.
- Identify and analyze authors' use of language.
- Compile appropriate examples of persuasion and language manipulation.
- Make a convincing, logical presentation to class.
- Identify techniques helpful to the consumer.

PERFORMANCE TASK II:

Magazines and newspapers are filled with advertisements persuading people to buy products and services. Cut out a number of examples and determine which language techniques are used to manipulate people. Design an advertisement for a product using a specific language persuasion technique. Present your advertisement to your classmates and have them identify and explain your technique. Explain how consumers could benefit from understanding the technique you used.

Language Arts:
Grade 12

Performance
Benchmark

READING
CONTENT/CONCEPT STANDARDS 1, 4, 6

KEY ORGANIZING QUESTION:

How can one theme have so many interpretations?

KEY COMPETENCES	KEY CONCEPTS AND CONTENT	PERFORMANCE TASKS
Locate Interpret Analyze Compare Expand Present	Compare themes in different genres. Analyze and appreciate different interpretations.	**PERFORMANCE TASK I:** As part of your class study of a theme on human conflict, you will present an oral and visual presentation to a local civic or service group or a history class in your school. Using a variety of genres, your presentation might include examples of conflict between nations, social classes, ethnic groups, men and women, historical periods, and generations. In your presentation, be sure to address these questions: What makes people argue or fight? What contributes to their differences? What can we do to understand one another better? How can we overcome conflicts?

PERFORMANCE TASK II:
Love is a theme that permeates the lives and literature of all cultures. Design and develop an oral presentation for the ninth-grade literature class that captures the different interpretations of "love" using references from a variety of different genres (e.g., biography, movie, diary, poetry, novel, essay). Have the class respond by brainstorming current-day examples and comparing them with examples from literature (e.g., Is there a modern day example of the theme addressed in *Romeo and Juliet*?).

QUALITY CRITERIA:
"LOOK FORS"
• Locate examples of themes from a variety of genres.
• Analyze and interpret the treatment of a theme.
• Compare the treatment of the theme in a different genre.
• Explain the meaning and treatment of the theme in an organized presentation and product.

VIEWING AND REPRESENTING

Content/Concept Standards

In the technoinformation age, most of what we know beyond our immediate personal experiences comes to us through the media. This wouldn't present a problem if media simply reflected reality. However, what we are learning is that each medium of communication shapes reality in different ways. It is impossible for us to consider any message in any medium as being neutral or value-free. All the mass media contain messages about values, beliefs, and behaviors, and often these are influenced by economic factors.

Therefore, it is important that students learn to be media literate, which means they must be informed and critically understand the various forms of media, as well as the techniques, technologies, and beliefs involved in the production of media. Media literacy goes beyond reading and listening and involves viewing and interpreting visual messages. These messages are a major source of information in our society, and they have the power to influence our thinking and behavior.

Instructional Issues in Viewing and Representing

Students view the world around them from birth, but they need to become critical viewers and consumers of media texts. As part of their language development, they must acquire the ability to comprehend, interpret, and create a wide variety of media texts. It is essential that students are able to interpret information presented visually, orally, and electronically in order to see how it can shape reality and present biases. Issues such as stereotyping, power, and accuracy need to be studied and discussed.

Viewing and Representing Strategies

The emphasis in teaching viewing and representing is on the dynamic process of analyzing and constructing media texts. Through the experience of production strategies, students will recognize the control the producer has over the many messages, explicit and implicit, that are conveyed. The results related to this strand can be best achieved by students working in other discipline areas or in cross-curricular studies.

What all viewers and representers should know and be able to do

Recognize form and purpose:
- Select viewing materials from a wide range of forms (including a variety of electronic forms)
- Critically reflect on choices
- Closely examine the different media, forms of texts, and genres
- Match the selections to different audiences and purposes

Interpret and produce:
- Analyze the message in a media text
- Examine issues associated with social, racial, and cultural stereotyping in the media
- Identify and explain the method that is used to convey a message
- Develop production skills
- Construct texts to convey implicit and explicit meanings

Identify features and conventions of text:
- Identify codes and conventions used in media production
- Interpret and explain codes and conventions used in media production
- Produce media text according to accepted media codes and conventions

The strategies for viewing and representing are integral to the following performance benchmarks for each grade level.

What students should know how to do by the end of Grade 3

Students will view a wide variety of media texts for pleasure and information. They will relate their viewing to personal experiences and respond to the ideas being conveyed. They should identify elements that appeal to certain audiences and respond critically to the way ideas are presented. They should be able to construct a media text that represents their own ideas and reflect critically on its effectiveness. They should be able to

1. View a wide range of media text for information and enjoyment
2. Produce messages or reports for different audiences
3. Select the best form for presenting to a particular audience
4. Describe main characteristics that distinguish personal media forms of communication from commercial forms of communication intended for mass audiences
5. Distinguish between real and imaginary material in media texts
6. Question the content and methods they use in their productions
7. Seek responses and reviews of their work

What students should know how to do by the end of Grade 5

Students should continue to view a wider range of media texts for both entertainment and information. They should begin to model observed techniques and strategies in their own productions. They should begin to create productions for the purpose of influencing an audience. They should also begin to analyze the audience response to their work. They should be able to

1. Explore and use a wide range of media texts for entertainment and information
2. Incorporate a wider range of forms in their own productions
3. Identify and analyze the ways in which program content and commercials on television are geared to a targeted audience
4. Describe how different elements in media texts help to create atmosphere and shape meaning
5. Ask questions about the intended message of media text
6. State opinions about the content of observed productions in terms of accuracy, relevance, and bias

What students should know how to do by the end of Grade 8

At this stage of development, students can make more personal connections and judgments about media texts. They can easily discern concrete meanings and most abstract meanings. They attend more closely to the audience and the planned message when they create productions. They should be able to

1. Identify and use an extensive range of media text as sources of information
2. Display a wide variety of forms in production efforts
3. Display a wide variety of techniques related to production
4. Identify the sources of revenue for various types of television programs and other electronic media presentations
5. Compare and contrast the ways in which different media present the same topic or story
6. Identify implicit as well as explicit messages and biases in media texts
7. Critically examine the reactions of others to a range of media texts
8. Choose an appropriate medium and form for plans of an individual or group production
9. Explore issues of stereotyping in the media through group viewing and discussion
10. Supply supporting evidence on the effectiveness of key elements used in a media text

What students should know how to do by the end of Grade 12

By this stage of development, the student should demonstrate complex skills in the viewing of sophisticated media texts and forms. They should be able to make insightful connections between the elements or techniques and the message. They should generate keen understandings of how audience response to content can affect sponsorship and continuing sales or advertising. They should confidently make judgments and offer strong supporting evidence on the effectiveness of topic presentation in media text. They should be able to

1. Integrate form and technique to plan and create innovative productions

2. Use complex and sophisticated media texts to locate and analyze specific information about political, economic, social, and cultural issues in this country and the world

3. Produce innovative productions that anticipate and motivate viewer response

4. Select from a variety of forms the best way to present an issue to obtain a particular audience response

5. Analyze and interpret meaning implied in media text

6. Develop insightful connections between the elements or techniques of production and the message

7. Connect personal understanding and perspective of bias and stereotyping to general social issues and events

8. Evaluate structure, content, and aesthetics of a media text and the effectiveness of the production

9. Incorporate a complex variety of sources to support the interpretation and point of view expressed in a production

10. Explore sources of revenue for various types of media presentations

11. Explain consequences of sponsorship for program content

Language Arts:
Grade 3

Performance
Benchmark

VIEWING AND REPRESENTING
CONTENT/CONCEPT STANDARDS 5, 7

KEY ORGANIZING QUESTION:

How can you tell the difference between real and imaginary ideas in media materials?

KEY COMPETENCES	KEY CONCEPTS AND CONTENT	PERFORMANCE TASKS
Review Select Plan Create Practice Present	Distinguish between realistic and imaginary materials in media treatment.	**PERFORMANCE TASK I:** The power company wants all citizens to understand the danger of fallen electrical lines. Your class will review different media approaches to this topic (TV, movies, cartoons, newspaper). Select the message you want to deliver to the kindergartners. Plan visual representations that depict the message in (a) a serious way and (b) a humorous (or imaginary) way. Present your visual messages and ask the students what they have learned from them. Be sure to explain the difference between real and imaginary circumstances.

PERFORMANCE TASK II:
There are many examples of unsafe situations in many of our home environments. Your class will review different media examples of these unsafe situations. Select one example and depict it seriously and humorously. Explain the difference. Present your safety depictions to another class. Ask the class what the presentations mean to them.

QUALITY CRITERIA:
"LOOK FORS"

- Identify the purpose of your visual representation.
- Select two different views to depict.
- Develop a plan or sketch.
- Carefully create your visual representation.
- Practice and present an organized message.

Language Arts:
Grade 5

VIEWING AND REPRESENTING
CONTENT/CONCEPT STANDARDS 3, 4

KEY ORGANIZING QUESTION:

How do the method and text in a message influence the audience?

KEY COMPETENCES	KEY CONCEPTS AND CONTENT	PERFORMANCE TASKS
Observe Identify Analyze Design Develop Predict Present Survey	How program content and commercials are geared to a targeted audience. Elements that create atmosphere and shape meaning.	**PERFORMANCE TASK I:** Observe and analyze the methods and text of several popular media messages (e.g., how cat lovers respond to the use of cute cats in commercials for unrelated products). Identify different types of messages and analyze how the audience is influenced by them. Design and develop a commercial for a particular audience. Predict the response of your audience. Present your commercial, and survey your audiences afterward to learn their reactions. How well did you predict your audience's reactions? What should you change?

QUALITY CRITERIA:
"LOOK FORS"

- Identify your purpose for observing.
- Select the main targets of impact.
- Compare and contrast the effect of these techniques.
- Identify an audience and message.
- Map out your plan.
- Create the media presentation including three special techniques.
- Predict the audience response.
- Present according to identified conventions for audience.
- Survey the audience reaction.
- Record and compare with other attempts.

PERFORMANCE TASK II:

Review the results of the above commercial. Redesign it for a different audience. How can you adjust the mood, sequence, focus, and use of techniques to accomplish your purpose with a totally different audience? Try it again. Compare the results with your first attempt.

VIEWING AND REPRESENTING
CONTENT/CONCEPT STANDARDS 2, 6, 7

KEY ORGANIZING QUESTION:

How can a producer influence the emotions and response of the viewer?

KEY COMPETENCES	KEY CONCEPTS AND CONTENT	PERFORMANCE TASKS
Observe Analyze Select Plan Explain Create	Implicit and explicit messages and biases in media text. Reactions of others. Medium and form in planning for a production.	**PERFORMANCE TASK I:** Observe and analyze three to five media text examples that contain concrete and abstract meaning. Analyze the abstract messages and identify point of view in the text. Explain how the content, techniques, and intent of the producer can influence the emotions and response of the viewer (e.g., special camera angles, use of black and white only, or oppressive background music). Select an appropriate medium, form, and topic. Plan a production using abstract and concrete messages. Use a storyboard to lay out your script. Clearly explain your intent as a producer. Create your production. Present it to a selected audience, and survey them for reactions to your intent.

PERFORMANCE TASK II:

Observe your production as you show it to several different audiences. Write a review of the production. Be sure to evaluate the structure, content, and aesthetics. Evaluate the effectiveness of your use of concrete and abstract messages. Use a variety of sources to support your interpretation and the point of view you projected.

QUALITY CRITERIA:
"LOOK FORS"

• Observe text examples for concrete and abstract meaning.
• Analyze by comparing and contrasting effectiveness of examples.
• Identify and explain the producer's intent.
• Select a topic, appropriate medium, and form.
• Lay out a script.
• Develop the production.
• Survey audience response.
• Reflect on your accomplishments.
• Review the process.

Language Arts: **Performance**
Grade 12   **Benchmark**

VIEWING AND REPRESENTING
CONTENT/CONCEPT STANDARDS 9, 10, 11

KEY ORGANIZING QUESTION:

What effect can sponsors have on issues and positions taken in some media texts?

KEY COMPETENCES	KEY CONCEPTS AND CONTENT	PERFORMANCE TASKS
Interview Interpret Design Create Present Reflect	Revenue sources for media presentations. Sponsor effects on program content. Point of view.	**PERFORMANCE TASK I:** Interview a representative from an advertising firm. Question the representative to learn how certain companies attach their advertising to specific kinds of media texts or events. Find out what the revenue sources can be for certain texts or events. Ask for information on sponsor influence on issues and positions presented in texts or programs. Also see if you can learn how important audience reaction to the content is for the sponsor. Interpret the data from your interview; then design and create a media script for a documentary on how this information affects a media producer. You could share your documentary with future students in this class. You might also see if a cable channel would be interested in broadcasting your documentary. **PERFORMANCE TASK II:** Interview a marketing officer from a major company. Use the topics identified above for gathering information from this different perspective. Interpret the data you collect and compare it with the advertising perspective. Would your documentary still be satisfactory, or should you make revisions based on the new information? If additions are needed, plan them and then create your new documentary. Review it with classmates and seek a distributor.

QUALITY CRITERIA:
"LOOK FORS"

• Establish clear goals for your interview.
• Prepare clear, concise questions.
• Select the most appropriate information for your purpose.
• Create a storyboard for your documentary.
• Expand the major points for presenting.
• Organize the details for production.
• Create the documentary.
• Review with fellow students.
• Solicit a distributor for your media product.

2
TECHNOLOGY CONNECTIONS

SUMMARY

Why Address Technology in a Performance-Based Curriculum?

A performance-based curriculum starts with the understanding that students will make use of what they learn in the production and dissemination of knowledge. Technology is revolutionizing the way we access information; the capabilities we have in interpreting and analyzing data; the methods by which we produce, design, and construct products resulting from our learning; the forms those products take; the methods by which the products are disseminated; and the evaluation procedures we can undertake. *Access, interpret, produce, disseminate,* and *evaluate:* These are the five central learning actions in a performance-based curriculum. These learning actions used in conjunction with technology give the learner more power and lead to greater effectiveness.

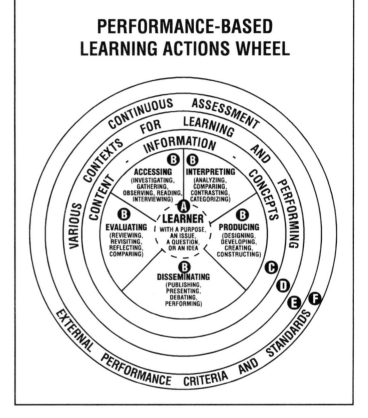

PERFORMANCE-BASED LEARNING ACTIONS WHEEL

Technology as Content

Our physical, social, and material worlds are being radically changed as a result of the explosion of new technologies. Technological change and the issues stemming from that change provide content that is increasingly addressed in the study of history, economics, political science, and other disciplines making up the social sciences. They are also subject matter for novels, science fiction, and political and social essays. Technology is a central focus of futuristic studies. It is a product of, as well as a critical ingredient in, modern science. Technological developments have radically altered the tools used by authors and everyone involved in communication and the use of language. Technology is a rich source of topics for integrating a performance-based curriculum.

Technology as a Tool

Technology is also used as a tool in a performance-based curriculum. Although technology can be used as a way of controlling the learner's interaction with the curriculum, technology is most appropriately used as a tool controlled by the learner in the performance-based approach to learning. It is that approach that is applied in correlating this section with the Language Arts section.

Many technologies can enhance a performance-based curriculum. Their common characteristic is that they are tools that improve communication of and access to multimedia data (words, numbers, sounds, still and motion pictures, still and motion graphics) and make the use of those data easier and more effective. In a perfect world, every student and teacher would have a workstation equipped with a computer, modem, CD-ROM, laserdisc player, and a videotape camera and player. This workstation would be connected to networks that allow access to multimedia data on demand. The networks would distribute information in multimedia format to others throughout the world. In addition to these workstations, teachers and learners would have access to copying, scanning, and printing machines; CD-ROM presses; video editing equipment; audio recording and editing equipment; and software to support writing, computer-aided design, statistics, graphing, musical and artistic productions, and so on. Additional equipment would be found in a science laboratory, including tools for specialized data collection and analysis. In other specialty areas, such as art, lithographic presses would be available. Drafting equipment, electronic tools, and other specialized technologies would be present where necessary to allow the teaching of those technological subject areas.

Technology is a tool (among other tools) useful for acquiring, storing, manipulating, and communicating information in a multimedia format. Technology will be used to gather data, explore questions, produce products, and communicate results.

Technology in Support of Learning Actions

Five learning actions are central to a performance-based curriculum: **ACCESS**, **INTERPRET**, **PRODUCE**, **DISSEMINATE**, and **EVALUATE**. Throughout this curriculum framework, the use of appropriate technologies will support students in being active learners. Students will be encouraged to use technology to generate questions and identify problems in a wide variety of contexts; formulate hypotheses and generate tentative solutions to the questions or the problems they have defined; test the reasonableness of their answers and respond to challenges to their positions; reach a conclusion about an issue, a problem, or a question and use that "solution" as a jumping-off place to ask other questions; and engage in the learning process again.

A learner with a purpose, an issue, a question, or an idea needs to be able to use appropriate technologies in carrying out these learning actions. Technology is especially important in accessing information, producing products, and disseminating the results of one's work. We organize the benchmarks of the skills students must have in using technology around these key learning actions that can take full advantage of current technologies: **ACCESS**, **PRODUCE**, and **DISSEMINATE**. Examples have been developed for some strands at each of the grade levels. Each example contains suggestions on how to use technology to **ACCESS** information, **PRODUCE** products, and **DISSEMINATE** the results of one's efforts. These examples are meant to stimulate and facilitate the mastery of the use of appropriate technologies in the pursuit of learning. The suggested technologies encompass a broad range of tools useful in accessing, producing, and disseminating data that are not just words and numbers but are also sounds, still and motion graphics, and still and motion pictures. Students and teachers are encouraged to use all appropriate tools and disseminate their products using a combination of technologies.

Technology changes rapidly. The skills and abilities described below require modification on a regular basis to reflect the latest technologies. These skills and abilities must be understood as dynamic objectives rather than as static goals. They are essential learning actions that increase the student's ability to **ACCESS**, **PRODUCE**, and **DISSEMINATE**.

SKILLS AND ABILITIES

How students should be able to use technology by the end of Grade 3

Access:

A1   Gather information with still, digital, or video camera

A2   Search databases to locate information

A3   Gather sounds and conversations with audio and video recorders

A4   Collect digitized audio data

A5   Access information on laserdisc by using bar code reader

A6   Scan to capture graphic data

A7   Copy to gather graphics

A8   Retrieve and print information using a computer

A9   Gather information through telephone

A10 Select and use information from CDs

A11 Fax to send and receive printed information

A12 Identify and use all types of materials, such as print, nonprint, and electronic media

A13 Locate information using electronic indexes or media

Produce:

P1   Draw and paint graphics and pictures using a computer

P2   Create flip card animations using a computer

P3   Design and develop computer products including pictures, text, flip card animations, sounds, and graphics

P4   Design and develop audiotapes

P5   Design and develop videotapes

P6   Create overhead or slide presentations with or without background music

P7   Develop stories using computer-generated text with either handmade or computer-generated illustrations

Disseminate:

D1   Present *Logo* or *HyperCard* (or similar) computer product including pictures, text, flip card animations, sounds, and graphics

D2   Publish printed page including text and graphics

D3   Broadcast audiotape

D4   Broadcast videotape

D5   Present overhead or slide presentation

D6   Fax information to other audiences

D7   Explain products or creations to an audience

How students should be able to use technology by the end of Grade 5

Access:

A1 Gather information with a still, digital, or video camera of moderate complexity

A2 Gather information using text-based databases to locate information

A3 Access information on laserdisc by using bar code reader and computer controls

A4 Gather information using telephone and modem to connect to other users and databases (Internet, eWorld, etc.)

A5 Search basic library technologies for data

A6 Select and use specialized tools appropriate to grade level and subject matter

A7 Record interviews with experts

A8 Scan CD collections for needed information

Produce:

P1 Create path-based animations using computer

P2 Create with computer painting and drawing tools of moderate complexity

P3 Digitize still and motion pictures

P4 Create basic spreadsheet for addition, subtraction, multiplication, and division

P5 Graph data (pie charts, line and bar graphs) using computer

P6 Create edited videotapes of moderate complexity using a videotape editing deck or computer-based digital editing system or two connected cassette recorders (VCRs)

P7 Input text into computer using keyboard with appropriate keyboard skills

P8 Design and develop moderately complex *Logo* or *HyperCard* (or similar) programs including pictures, sounds, flip card and path-based animations, graphics, text, and motion pictures

P9 Design and develop multipage document including text and graphics using computer

P10 Create edited audiotape

P11 Create edited videotape

P12 Create overhead or slide presentation with synchronized voice narration with or without background music

P13 Layout advertisements, posters, and banners

Disseminate:

D1 Present moderately complex *Logo* or *HyperCard* (or similar) computer product including pictures, sounds, flip card and path-based animations, graphics, text, and motion pictures

D2 Publish multipage printed document including formatted, paginated text and graphics

D3 Broadcast edited audiotape and videotape

D4 Present programs using overhead projector, slide projector, or computer

D5 Present information over public address system in a school, community, or meeting situation

D6 Display information in a variety of formats

D7 Advertise for events, services, or products

D8 Broadcast performances and products

D9 Broadcast on cable TV

How students should be able to use technology by the end of Grade 8

Access:

A1   Gather information using computer, CD-ROM, and laserdisc databases

A2   Gather data using telephone and modem (including graphics and sounds) to and from other users and databases (Internet, eWorld, etc.)

A3   Search basic spreadsheet and databasing software for "what if?" comparisons and analyses

A4   Search technologies for accessing data outside the school and local library

A5   Search menus to locate information on computer software, CD-ROM, or laserdiscs

A6   Video interviews

A7   Download information from Internet

Produce:

P1   Create products using computer painting and drawing tools, including moderately complex color tools

P2   Digitize still and motion pictures

P3   Create edited videotapes by using a videotape editing deck or computer-based digital editing system

P4   Create computer presentation program

P5   Develop cell-based animations using computer

P6   Design and develop complex *Logo* or *HyperCard* (or similar) programs including still pictures; flip card, path-based, and cell-based animations; sounds; graphics; and motion pictures

P7   Create multipage documents including text and graphics using computer page layout tools

P8   Develop audiotapes that combine sounds and voice data from a variety of sources

P9   Produce videotapes that are organized, coherent, and well edited

P10   Create a personal database requiring the collection of data over time

Disseminate:

D1   Present relatively complex *Logo* or *HyperCard* (or similar) product including still pictures; flip card, path-based, and cell-based animations; sounds; graphics; and motion pictures

D2   Publish multipage printed documents including text and graphics

D3   Broadcast edited audiotape of moderate complexity

D4   Broadcast edited videotape of moderate complexity

D5   Broadcast video presentation over schoolwide Channel 1 (Whittle), citywide public Channel 28, or citywide ITFS schools-only equipment

D6   Advertise events, services, or products

D7   Display information and designs on various formats available

D8   Broadcast on closed circuit or cable television

D9   Broadcast filmed and live performances on television

D10   Distribute over available sources in Internet

How students should be able to use technology by the end of Grade 12

Access:

A1   Access and use complex electronic databases and communication networks of all types including, but not limited to, Internet

A2   Research using sensors, probes, and other specialized scientific tools as appropriate

A3   Gather information from spreadsheet, databasing software, and statistical packages, including the use of formulas and charting routines

A4   Search technologies for data and primary sources (publications and persons)

A5   Identify local, regional, and national databases and procedures for needed data

A6   Review online bulletin boards, databases, and electronic retrieval services for data

Produce:

P1   Create with complex computer painting and drawing tools and programs

P2   Create 3-D graphics using drawing and modeling tools

P3   Create changing images using computer digital-morphing programs

P4   Illustrate concrete and abstract concepts using computer-aided design and mathematical modeling

P5   Create CD-ROM simulations

P6   Create complex cell-based animations, including 3-D objects, using the computer

P7   Create complex *Logo* or *HyperCard* (or similar) programs including pictures; flip card, path-based, and cell-based animations; sounds; 3-D graphics; and motion pictures

P8   Develop multipage documents with information from a variety of sources, including text and graphics using appropriate computer page layout tools

P9   Create documents using a variety of fonts and type faces

P10   Assemble findings based on spreadsheets, databasing software, and statistical packages involving the use of formulas as appropriate

P11   Design graphic and text titles for digital video productions

P12   Develop digitally edited materials including audio, motion pictures, still-frame pictures, motion graphics, and still-frame graphics

P13   Design and develop a personal database of moderate complexity

P14   Illustrate concrete and abstract mathematical and scientific concepts

P15   Assemble information by creating, searching, and sorting databases

P16   Design and develop a dissemination design for video using ITFS microwave and satellite up-and-down links

Disseminate:

D1   Transmit complex *Logo* or *HyperCard* (or similar) computer product including pictures; flip card, path-based, and cell-based animations; sounds; 3-D graphics; and motion pictures

D2   Publish multipage printed documents, appropriately laid out, including text and graphics

D3   Transmit complex spreadsheet or database findings

D4   Telecast digital video product of some complexity

D5   Present computer-based animation program (cell- or path-based animations, or both)

D6   Publish reports generated from database searches

D7   Publish scientific investigations and results or recommendations

D8   Transmit a video presentation to secondary students using ITFS microwave, Whittle Channel 1 equipment, public Channel 28, cable hookups, and satellite up-and-down links to local schools or students in other school systems

Technology Connections
Language Arts: Grade 3

SPEAKING
CORRESPONDING PERFORMANCE BENCHMARK, PAGE 26

KEY ORGANIZING QUESTION:

How can you use a skit to convey an important message?

ACCESS	PRODUCE	DISSEMINATE
PERFORMANCE TASK I: You are a member of a team that is preparing a skit about "Saying No to Drugs" that you will video-tape and show to other third-grade classes in your school. As part of the preparation for your script, you must find information about how to encourage others to "Say No to Drugs." Make a list of community groups that can help provide you with that information. Call them for information. In addition, use appropriate library sources to gather information for your skit.	**PERFORMANCE TASK I:** Generate your script on a word processing program. Videotape your rehearsals and critique changes. Videotape your final presentation.	**PERFORMANCE TASK I:** Present your videotape to other third-grade classes.
PERFORMANCE TASK II: You are a member of a team that is preparing a skit designed to convince kindergarten students to eat healthy foods. You want to include pictures on your skit. Using a regular camera, take pictures of healthy foods.	**PERFORMANCE TASK II:** Create close-up enlargements of pictures of healthy foods. Zoom in on these pictures during your filming.	**PERFORMANCE TASK II:** Present your videotape to the kindergarten classes.

**Technology Connections
Language Arts: Grade 5**

**Performance
Benchmark**

SPEAKING
CORRESPONDING PERFORMANCE BENCHMARK, PAGE 27

KEY ORGANIZING QUESTION:

Can you persuade others to accept your conclusions about an issue?

ACCESS	PRODUCE	DISSEMINATE
PERFORMANCE TASK I: You are to collect data on the number of hours students watch TV and the number of hours they exercise in 1 week. Enter your data into a spreadsheet as you collect it. Examine the data and make comparisons.	**PERFORMANCE TASK I:** Using your computer, generate appropriate graphs that demonstrate the relationship (if any) between TV watching and exercising. Print the graphs on transparencies. If you have plain paper copies, enlarge them for others to see easily.	**PERFORMANCE TASK I:** Using the graphs that you have produced, make a presentation to your class. Share your conclusions about the relationship (if any) between TV watching and exercising. Try to get your classmates to accept your conclusions.
PERFORMANCE TASK II: You are to collect data about what students in your class eat for lunch. Enter these data into a spreadsheet or appropriate database. Also enter into your database an approved nutritious diet. Compare the nutritious standard with what your fellow students actually eat.	**PERFORMANCE TASK II:** Prepare appropriate graphs and charts dealing with what students eat and comparing students with each other. Produce graphs and charts comparing what students eat with nutritious standard. Make sure that your graphs and charts make clear the deviations that exist between what should be eaten by your classmates and what they are actually eating. Print the graphs and charts on transparencies or enlarge the copies so others can easily see them.	**PERFORMANCE TASK II:** Using the graphs and charts you have produced, make a presentation to your class advocating healthy eating habits. Be convincing. Check to see how many classmates accept your argument.

Technology Connections
Language Arts: Grade 8

SPEAKING
CORRESPONDING PERFORMANCE BENCHMARK, PAGE 28

KEY ORGANIZING QUESTION:

What questions about a career are most important, and how can people learn about a particular career?

ACCESS	PRODUCE	DISSEMINATE
PERFORMANCE TASK I: You are working as a member of a team developing a panel presentation on careers. You are to answer questions raised by your audience, and you are to conduct a survey of the members of your audience after the panel discussion and the question-and-answer period are completed. Because several audiences (other classes in your school) cannot attend your live panel presentation, you will videotape it. You still want to answer questions. You will do this in several ways. First, members of the other class can telephone you with questions. Keep a log of all telephone inquiries received. Second, the members of the other audiences can send you electronic questions. You will reply to these electronic questions. Third, some audiences may be able to transmit video and audio images to your classroom, and you may be able to do the same using Channel 1 or closed-circuit television. If so, you can deal with questions in the same manner as you deal with the questions from your "live" audience. On a word processor, prepare the questionnaire that will accompany your presentation.	**PERFORMANCE TASK I:** Produce a videotape of your panel presentation. Print the questionnaire that will accompany the presentation.	**PERFORMANCE TASK I:** Distribute the videotape of the panel presentation to other classes. Respond to telephone questions and electronic messages and questions. Distribute your questionnaire and arrange for its completion and return by the members of your distant audiences. Publish the results.
PERFORMANCE TASK II: You are to prepare a radio or TV commercial recruiting others to a career that you have chosen. Gather the data necessary to prepare your commercial. Make any drawings, scan any pictures, record any interviews, and collect any other information that you will need. Prepare a storyboard for your commercial. Prepare a response sheet that gathers feedback on your audience's interest in your career using a ranking of 1 (highest) to 5 (lowest).	**PERFORMANCE TASK II:** Record your commercial on either audiotape or videotape. Edit it. Print the response form that you will use to solicit feedback from your audience.	**PERFORMANCE TASK II:** Distribute your audio or visual commercial. Arrange for its "broadcast." Devise a way to distribute the feedback form that you have prepared. Collect the feedback form. Analyze the responses. What information do they give you about the effectiveness of your advertisement? Publish your conclusions.

Technology Connections
Language Arts: Grade 12

**Performance
Benchmark**

SPEAKING
CORRESPONDING PERFORMANCE BENCHMARK, PAGE 29

KEY ORGANIZING QUESTION:

What speaking techniques are most effective to persuade others concerning social and political issues?

ACCESS	PRODUCE	DISSEMINATE
PERFORMANCE TASK I: You are to engage in a debate concerning political and social issues about which there is disagreement. The rules of the debate allow you to use the very short audio or video clips of contemporary songs. These clips can be used to identify issues or provide support for your position. To be useful, they must be edited so that they are very short and to the point. In addition, they must be indexed so that they can be quickly retrieved and shown to your audience. You have decided that you will use *HyperCard*, or another appropriate computer tool, that can index and instantly access audio and video clips. You will use your computer to play these clips. A video projection unit must be attached to your computer in order to show video clips.	**PERFORMANCE TASK I:** Gather and edit audio and video clips. Digitize the clips. Create the *HyperCard* index. Test its use.	**PERFORMANCE TASK I:** Access and use the clips in your debate and in any responses in which you engage.
PERFORMANCE TASK II: Using advanced library search techniques, as well as search procedures for local, regional, and national electronic databases, create a list of political and social issues that are dealt with in literature. Enter the data you collect into an appropriate database that you have constructed. Generate a list of issues on which different authors take opposing views. Select one issue for debate with another student. Using appropriate computer software, prepare a survey instrument for use by your audience at the conclusion of the debate.	**PERFORMANCE TASK II:** Produce a printout of the list of issues on which different authors take opposing views. Print your survey instrument.	**PERFORMANCE TASK II:** Use the printout of the list of issues on which different authors take opposing views to make a selection of a topic for debate. Distribute the survey instrument to your audience and collect the data at the conclusion of your debate. Analyze the findings of your survey.

Technology Connections
Language Arts: Grade 3

Performance
Benchmark

READING
CORRESPONDING PERFORMANCE BENCHMARK, PAGE 42

KEY ORGANIZING QUESTION:

How do we find information to increase our knowledge and understanding of the past?

ACCESS	PRODUCE	DISSEMINATE
PERFORMANCE TASK I: You are working (as a member of a team) on a book about what was happening in your community, the United States, and the world 50 years ago. You have decided that your team will produce a book that, in addition to having words and pictures, also has sounds in it. Using the library, the telephone, the school fax machine, and electronic bulletin boards, locate sounds that will be useful for your book. These sounds might also be on laserdiscs, old records, CDs (such as those on American history, or the CD entitled *Great Speeches*) or videotapes. (Some famous movies are now more than 50 years old.) Using your computer as a recording device, or using an audiotape recorder, record some sounds that you can use in your book.	**PERFORMANCE TASK I:** Organize your book. If it is to be printed, devise a way to include your sounds (such as including an audiotape). If your book is to be an electronic book, use *HyperCard* or some other appropriate tool to "print" your book on a computer disk or disks. Include your sounds.	**PERFORMANCE TASK I:** Distribute your book to your classmates. If the book is printed and there is an audiotape included, encourage your fellow students to "listen" to your book. If your book is printed on computer disks, get your class-mates to "read" the book using the computer. If you got help from anyone in preparing your book, be sure to inform them how they can get a copy or where they can come to "read" your book.
PERFORMANCE TASK II: You are working on a scrapbook describing what has happened in your community and around the country a hundred years ago. Locate pictures of your community or of the United State that will help illustrate your book. Use all of the resources of your school library. In addition, telephone the local pub-lic library and any other appropriate sources in your community. If any of the people or organizations whom you call have materials that could be useful to you, have them send you copies by mail, by fax, by Internet, or over other electronic networks. Scan any pictures into your computer. Prepare your text using the word processor.	**PERFORMANCE TASK II:** Organize the scrapbook containing the materials that you have found.	**PERFORMANCE TASK II:** Make copies of your scrapbook. Distribute them to the members of your class. Send a fax to anyone who faxed you materials, telling them about your book and how they can request a copy. Write or call all others who provided you assis-tance and inform them of how they can request a copy of the book pro-duced by your group.

**Technology Connections
Language Arts: Grade 5**

**Performance
Benchmark**

READING
CORRESPONDING PERFORMANCE BENCHMARK, PAGE 43

KEY ORGANIZING QUESTION:

How do I understand people who are different from me?

ACCESS	PRODUCE	DISSEMINATE
PERFORMANCE TASK I: You are working on a magazine for a new classmate from a different culture. The new magazine compares your culture with that of your new classmate. You are making an electronic edition of the magazine that includes pictures (still and motion) and sounds, as well as print. Using your library, locate relevant materials. You might also contact other students living in areas with a culture like that of your new classmate. Contact them by Internet or over another electronic network. Get their help in identifying cultural differences. You might want to include short recordings of popular songs that reflect cultural differences, recordings of speech differences, copies of works of art that demonstrate cultural differences, or other data that would be useful in the electronic edition of your magazine.	**PERFORMANCE TASK I:** Publish your electronic magazine using *Hyper-Card* or some other appropriate computer tool. Gather your material together and organize it into an interesting and exciting product that will appeal to your new classmate.	**PERFORMANCE TASK I:** Establish a computer station where your electronic magazine can be read. Be available to answer questions or provide other assistance as your new classmate and other classmates read your electronic magazine. Discuss your findings about cultural differences.
PERFORMANCE TASK II: You are to gather information about the traditions and lifestyles of a Native American tribe that once lived in your area of the county. Because you will be making a presentation to your class, you will want to have pictures to accompany your presentation. Use all of the resources in your library and other resources in your community to locate appropriate materials. Use the telephone, the fax machine, and electronic networks and bulletin boards to locate materials. Photograph places in your community that would make your report more interesting, and use a computer to draw maps or pictures for your report.	**PERFORMANCE TASK II:** Create overheads for your presentation, or arrange to project your report (if done on the computer) using the overhead projection device. If you are doing the latter, prepare your report in *HyperCard* or use another appropriate tool on your computer.	**PERFORMANCE TASK II:** Make your presentation to your class using an overhead projector, the overhead projector for your computer, or a portable computer with a screen that can be played on the overhead projector.

Technology Connections
Language Arts: Grade 8

READING
CORRESPONDING PERFORMANCE BENCHMARK, PAGE 44

KEY ORGANIZING QUESTION:
Should we believe everything we read and see?

ACCESS	PRODUCE	DISSEMINATE
PERFORMANCE TASK I: You are to analyze advertisements (print and TV) for the committee on consumer awareness that you have joined. You are to make a presentation informing consumers how advertisements manipulate language. In your presentation you will show examples of both print and TV advertisements. You will either present using a computer and an overhead projection device or using an overhead projector and a videotape player. In either case, you will have to locate and tape appropriate examples. Edit the TV examples to an appropriate length.	**PERFORMANCE TASK I:** Either digitize the example of the TV ads and scan copies of the print ads into the computer, or make copies of the print ads for overheads and edit the TV ads into one videotape with appropriate stopping points.	**PERFORMANCE TASK I:** Make your presentation to your class using an overhead projection device for your computer.
PERFORMANCE TASK II: You are to design a TV advertisement using a specific language technique. Create a storyboard for your ad.	**PERFORMANCE TASK II:** Record your advertisement on videotape. Edit it as appropriate.	**PERFORMANCE TASK II:** Show your TV ad to your class using the video projection equipment. Have the class identify the language techniques you used in your ad. Discuss their reactions and explain your techniques.

Technology Connections
Language Arts: Grade 12

**Performance
Benchmark**

READING
CORRESPONDING PERFORMANCE BENCHMARK, PAGE 45

KEY ORGANIZING QUESTION:

How can one theme have so many interpretations?

ACCESS	PRODUCE	DISSEMINATE
PERFORMANCE TASK I: You are to prepare a presentation for a local lawyers' association on "One person's justice is another person's punishment." You will have to gather materials from a variety of sources. Use all available resources in your library to locate materials. Contact potential sources over electronic networks. Search electronic bulletin boards and electronic data networks. After gathering materials you will use in your presentation (including pictures and audio and video data), organize the materials into a form that will clearly demonstrate the differences that are the focus of your presentation. Decide on at least one or two examples that would be appropriate for morphing (changing images into one another).	**PERFORMANCE TASK I:** Your presentation will be sent to the lawyers' association on videotape. A part of your presentation will be a videotape of you speaking. Other parts will be taped output from your computer where you have digitized appropriate pictures, animation, and video segments and where you have produced one or more morphed pictures. Produce and edit your tape for delivery to the lawyers' association. Be sure you include appropriate titles and credits your videotapes.	**PERFORMANCE TASK I:** Send your videotape to the lawyers' association. Also provide a copy of your videotape to your school or district television network (Channel 1 or Channel 28) for possible use by them. In addition, provide a copy of the videotape to your school library to be made available to other students studying justice and punishment.
PERFORMANCE TASK II: You are to prepare an oral or a visual presentation on a selected emotion to a ninth-grade class in your school. In preparation, you are to read about the selected emotion as interpreted in a variety of literary genres, including biographies, diaries, movies, poetry, novels, and essays. In order to make your presentation as interesting as possible, you have decided to make use of pictures and sound. You locate or draw appropriate pictures to accompany your presentation. You also record short poems about the emotion and edit video clips that are appropriate to your presentation.	**PERFORMANCE TASK II:** Prepare a multimedia presentation on the emotion you selected for the ninth-grade class using *HyperCard* or another appropriate computer presentation program	**PERFORMANCE TASK II:** Make your presentation to the ninth-grade class using the computer and the computer presentation equipment.

3
PERFORMANCE DESIGNERS

The ultimate key to success with performance-based education is the creativity, rigor, and consistency of focus that must characterize the ongoing instructional process in the classroom. Student success with the performance benchmarks identified in this text depends on daily interactions with the learning actions. Students must feel empowered to demonstrate the learning actions being taught so they can internalize them, take ownership, and apply them easily in the benchmark performances. They must be able to do this through a continuous improvement process with a focus on quality criteria.

In order to accomplish the performance benchmarks in this text, learners must have daily practice with the routine of learning and demonstrating through learning actions as they gain new understanding about concepts from the different disciplines. They must recognize that only through continuous improvement will they achieve the defined quality that must be their goal.

If this is to occur, teachers must design lessons specifically addressing the learning actions (access, interpret, produce, disseminate, and evaluate). Instruction on these learning actions will engage students in gathering and interpreting information so they can produce a product, service, or performance with their newly acquired insights and knowledge. Then they can disseminate or give their product, service, or performance to an authentic audience. They do all of these learning actions with a continuous focus on evaluating themselves and their work against the identified quality criteria that the teacher will be looking for.

The performance designer is a tool for teachers to use when planning for students to engage in a significant demonstration that is an interactive experience for students designed to include essential content, competence (learning actions), context (issue, situation, and audience), and quality criteria.

The completed performance designer will describe the total performance or demonstration of significance. All of the students' actions will be clearly stated. The teacher uses this performance designer to develop the necessary instructional sequences that will support the attainment of each of the desired actions. Once students know how to do the actions, they are ready to pursue the planned performance.

The following organizer provides an overview. Each major section in the planner is identified and corresponds to a detailed explanation that follows.

PERFORMANCE DESIGNER FORMAT

I

Ⓐ PURPOSE	What complex thinking process is the focus?	
Ⓑ KEY ORGANIZING QUESTION	An issue or challenge to investigate.	
Ⓒ ROLE	You are _____ who is expected to ...	

II

(Do what?)	*(With what?)*	*(How well?)*
Ⓓ Access and Ⓔ interpret by...	Ⓕ CONTENT/CONCEPTS	Ⓖ QUALITY CRITERIA "Look fors"

III

(In order to...	*...do what?)*	*(How well?)*
Ⓗ Produce by...	Ⓘ PRODUCT/ PERFORMANCE	Ⓙ QUALITY CRITERIA "Look fors"

IV

	(To/for whom? Where?)	*(How well?)*
Ⓚ Disseminate by...	Ⓛ AUDIENCE/ SETTING	Ⓜ QUALITY CRITERIA "Look fors"

Section I

The first section of the designer serves as an organizer for the key elements that follow.

PERFORMANCE DESIGNER ELEMENT	REFLECTIVE QUESTIONS
Ⓐ PURPOSE The reason the performance is worth doing. This section may be tied to state- or district-level assessment. It will more often relate to a complex thinking process that is the result of applied critical-reasoning skills. (Example: drawing a conclusion, making a recommendation)	What do I want to be sure students are more competent doing when this performance is complete? Do I want them to be able to develop a range of possible solutions to a problem? Will they investigate an issue from outside school, form an opinion, or describe and support a point of view? What complex thinking skill is the core purpose of this performance?
Ⓑ KEY ORGANIZING QUESTION As with the purpose, the question focuses and organizes the entire performance. It combines with the role and the audience to define the context.	What will the students be accessing information about? Do I want to select the issue or question to be accessed, or will the students determine the learning they will pursue? Is the question or issue developmentally appropriate, and can I facilitate obtaining the resources that students will need for the issue? Do the students have any experiential background for this issue? Will the experience be limited to learning from the experiences of others?
Ⓒ ROLE When students take on a role, the point of view of the role adds a dimension not common to most learning. The role introduces the prompt that initiates the entire performance.	Will this role be authentic? Or is it a role-play? For example, students as artists, authors, and investigators are real roles for students. Students as lawyers, policemen, or city council members do not have the same level of authenticity. They would be role-playing, which is pretending to be someone. Will there be more than one role or will students all be in the same role? How will I ensure that students will have a focused point of view to explore? In life outside school, who would answer this question or be concerned with this issue? What would that expert do? Who is the expert? What's the real role?

Section II

The second section of the performance designer focuses on having students carry out the learning actions of accessing and interpreting necessary content and concepts. The right-hand column of the top section defines the quality criteria, or "look fors," that will be taught, practiced, and assessed. These are the quality criteria of the performance benchmarks.

PERFORMANCE DESIGNER ELEMENT	REFLECTIVE QUESTIONS
Ⓓ ACCESS AND Accessing actions might require students to interview, locate, or read for information. The importance of student involvement in acquiring information requires a shift from teacher as information provider to teacher as facilitator for information accessing.	Where can information be accessed? Are there experts who can be interviewed? What publications will be helpful? Which texts contain related information? Who can we contact on the Internet? What other resources are available?
Ⓔ INTERPRET BY... *(Do what?)* Interpreting actions require students to review what they have collected and decide what it means now that they have it. Students may categorize the information they have, compare it with what they already know, and process it in a variety of critical and creative ways.	How will students interact with the information they have collected? Will they formulate new questions? Will they begin to be asked to draw conclusions or perhaps make predictions at this point in the performance? Who will students interact with to communicate their initial interpretations of the information? Will they have a peer conference? Will I ask questions or give answers?
Ⓕ CONTENT/CONCEPTS *(With what?)* This specifies the knowledge or information the students are to learn. The result at the end is only going to be as good as the information the students collect. The resources should go far beyond the text. The teacher should support with additional resources and literature examples.	What do the students need to know? Where will the information come from? What will be significant learning to retain after the performance is over? Why is it important for students to learn this? Where might they need to use it later? Next year? After they leave school? What connections can they make to other knowledge structures? What are different points of view?
Ⓖ QUALITY CRITERIA **("Look fors")** *(How well?)* Quality criteria are the specifications for the performance. It is critical that these "look fors" be observable and measurable and that they represent high-quality performances. The quality criteria stated in the third column will integrate the learning actions in the left-hand column with the content/concept to be learned in the center column.	What would an expert interviewer or artist do? What would be observable in the performance of a quality questioner or researcher? How would I know one if I saw one? Do the criteria match the learning action that has been selected, and do they describe a logical and relevant application of the content/concept that is to be learned?

Section III

The third main section on the performance designer is organized similarly but focuses on the producing action or competence in the Learning Actions Wheel. The middle column of this section allows the teacher to describe or specify the nature of the product or performance the students are to generate. The right-hand column describes the quality criteria, or "look fors," that pertain to that product or production.

PERFORMANCE DESIGNER ELEMENT	REFLECTIVE QUESTIONS
🄗 PRODUCE BY... *(In order to...* Producing actions ask students to synthesize their learning, to bring what has been learned together into a cohesive whole that has relevance. Students might design, build, develop, create, construct, or illustrate.	How will students bring what they have learned together? What actions will lead to a product and keep the students in the role? Are there stages to the producing action, such as design and develop or draft and write? What are the essential actions that will lead to a product?
🄘 PRODUCT/PERFORMANCE *...do what?)* This describes the product, service, or production that the student will address. It should be something that will benefit the authentic audience.	What would an expert create? How does this product relate to the required or identified knowledge base? How does this product incorporate the required skills? What impact should the product have on the audience?
🄙 QUALITY CRITERIA ("Look fors") *(How well?)* Quality criteria describe the learning actions as they occur in conjunction with the development of the product, service, or production. It is critical that the criteria be observable, and measurable, and that it represent quality.	What would an excellent product look like? How could it be described? Will the product or production indicate the designing and developing that were used? How can it be precisely described in relationship to the learning actions? What are the essential actions the student will perform that relate to the producing verbs?

Section IV

The last section of the performance designer relates to the disseminating learning actions. It describes the sharing of the product. The middle column of this section clearly denotes the *audience* and the *setting*, or *context*, in which the performance will occur. These factors are critical in determining the realistic impact of the student's learning. The right-hand column will describe the quality criteria for this portion of the performance designer by combining the disseminating action in relationship with the authentic audience. It defines the purpose for the learning.

PERFORMANCE DESIGNER ELEMENT	REFLECTIVE QUESTIONS
Ⓚ DISSEMINATE BY... Learning actions at this stage of the role performance or demonstration have the learners presenting their products, services, or productions. The form of the presentation will vary depending on the original purpose. The learner might disseminate by explaining, teaching, or dancing.	What will be the most efficient and effective form of communicating this new product? Will students choose to broadcast or publish or teach? How does this form best relate to the product and the purpose? How does this delivery relate to the role?
Ⓛ AUDIENCE/SETTING **(To/for whom? Where?)** The audience is the recipient of the learners' product or production. The degree of authenticity will be reflected in the composition of the audience. The setting for this performance could be related to the original issue being investigated as well as the purpose for this investigation, or the natural location of the recipient.	Who will benefit from the students' learning? Who can use this recommendation or this finding? Is it another learner? Someone at another grade level? Is it a team of engineers at General Motors? Or young patients in a dentist's office? Where is the audience?
Ⓜ QUALITY CRITERIA **("Look fors")** **(How well?)** The criteria describe the specification for delivering the product, service, or performance. They are observable and represent quality.	What does a quality presentation look like? What are the essential elements that clearly define a quality presentation? How do the criteria connect the disseminating actions with the learner and the audience?

The performance designer gives teachers a very useful tool for continuously defining learning in terms of a realistic role that students must either individually or collectively take on and accomplish. The performance designer also continuously engages students in the range of learning actions that successful people engage in after they graduate from school, but it does so in the safe environment of school under the careful guidance of the teacher. Learners will demonstrate each role performance according to their developmental level of growth. Continuous involvement and experience with learning actions and quality criteria will result in demonstrated student improvement and continuous upleveling of quality criteria that will fully prepare students for any performance benchmark they are asked to demonstrate.

EXAMPLES OF LEARNING ACTIONS

ACCESS:
Investigate
Gather
Interview
Research
Listen
Observe
Collect
Search
Inquire
Survey
View
Discover
Read
Explore
Examine

INTERPRET:
Analyze
Explain
Paraphrase
Rephrase
Clarify
Compare
Contrast
Summarize
Integrate
Evaluate
Translate
Prioritize
Synthesize
Sort
Classify

PRODUCE:
Create
Design
Develop
Draw
Write
Lay out
Build
Draft
Invent
Erect
Sketch
Assemble
Compose
Illustrate
Generate

DISSEMINATE:
Publish
Perform
Teach
Present
Transmit
Display
Explain
Broadcast
Act
Advertise
Discuss
Send
Sing
Dance
Telecast

EVALUATE:
Review
Reflect
Assess
Revisit
Compare
Conclude
Generalize
Prove
Question
Refute
Support
Verify
Test
Realign
Judge

SAMPLE PERFORMANCE DESIGNER FOR GRADE 3

PURPOSE:
To gather information and to make connections

- -

KEY ORGANIZING QUESTION:
What makes a story interesting?

- -

ROLE: *(You are ...)*
An investigative reporter

(Who is expected to ...)

COMPETENCE *(Do what?)*	CONTENT/CONCEPTS *(With what?)*	QUALITY CRITERIA *("Look fors")*
Access and interpret by ... interviewing and organizing and connecting	first-graders to learn what they were most frightened of or most worried about when they started school your gathered information by comparing their concerns with your own.	• Accurately identify your purpose. • Collect abundant information. • Sequentially organize the information. • Create connections by making a storyboard.

COMPETENCE *(In order to ...*	PRODUCT/PERFORMANCE *... do what?)*	QUALITY CRITERIA *("Look fors")*
Produce by ... creating	an article for a class newsletter on "Helping First Graders at Your School."	• Include messages that accurately describe the 1st-graders' concerns. • Write so the message can be clearly understood by the receiver/reader.

COMPETENCE	AUDIENCE / SETTING *(To/for whom? Where?)*	QUALITY CRITERIA *("Look fors")*
Disseminate by ... presenting and reading	the newsletter to the first-graders the article to their families.	• Read clearly. • Pace self appropriately. • Models appropriate behavior for first-graders.

SAMPLE PERFORMANCE DESIGNER FOR GRADE 5

PURPOSE:

To reach a conclusion and persuade others

KEY ORGANIZING QUESTION:

Can you persuade others to accept your conclusion about an issue?

ROLE: *(You are ...)*

An Olympic athlete

(Who is expected to ...)

COMPETENCE (Do what?)	CONTENT/CONCEPTS (With what?)	QUALITY CRITERIA ("Look fors")
Access and interpret by ... surveying and analyzing	an identified sample to learn habits of exercise and television watching the gathered information.	• Select sample targets for survey. • Contrast survey instructions. • Create graphs to depict information. • Explain the data.

COMPETENCE (In order to ...	PRODUCT/PERFORMANCE ... do what?)	QUALITY CRITERIA ("Look fors")
Produce by ... developing and defining	a presentation on the importance of physical exercise in one's personal schedule.	• Include all details, components, and comparisons.

COMPETENCE	AUDIENCE / SETTING (To/for whom? Where?)	QUALITY CRITERIA ("Look fors")
Disseminate by ... presenting	to a fourth-grade health or physical education class.	• Include appropriate visuals. • Speak clearly. • Respond to audience needs.

SAMPLE PERFORMANCE DESIGNER FOR GRADE 8

PURPOSE:
To make connections and analyze a person, place, situations, or position

LANGUAGE ARTS:
LISTENING
(SEE PAGE 20)

KEY ORGANIZING QUESTION:
What can be learned by being a critical listener?

ROLE: *(You are ...)*
Producer or news manager

(Who is expected to ...)

COMPETENCE *(Do what?)*	CONTENT/CONCEPTS *(With what?)*	QUALITY CRITERIA *("Look fors")*
Access and interpret by ... listening and analyzing	to different people who generate language for a specific audience (i.e., preacher, coach, newscaster, disc jockey) their delivery style, their purpose, their main ideas.	• Gather information from several different speakers. • Organize information in an orderly system. • Identify differences in style, purpose, and so on.

COMPETENCE *(In order to ...*	PRODUCT/PERFORMANCE *... do what?)*	QUALITY CRITERIA *("Look fors")*
Produce by ... designing and developing	a personal oral presentation for a specific group on a chosen topic with a clearly defined purpose and style.	• Identify audience. • Identify purpose for presentation. • Select appropriate style for delivery.

COMPETENCE	AUDIENCE / SETTING *(To/for whom? Where?)*	QUALITY CRITERIA *("Look fors")*
Disseminate by ... presenting	an oral presentation to the class.	• Audience can clearly identify purpose and style. • Audience then demonstrates or provides feedback that they do know or like what you intended.

SAMPLE PERFORMANCE DESIGNER FOR GRADE 12

PURPOSE:
To compare and contrast and then draw a conclusion

KEY ORGANIZING QUESTION:
How can one theme have so many interpretations?

ROLE: *(You are ...)*
A concerned citizen

(Who is expected to ...)

COMPETENCE (Do what?)	CONTENT/CONCEPTS (With what?)	QUALITY CRITERIA ("Look fors")
Access and interpret by ... investigating	justice and punishment practices of three cultures through history and literature	• Identify topic and audience. • Use a variety of credible, reliable resources. • Gather relevant information and concepts. • Choose an appropriate method for organizing big ideas and supporting details.
and analyzing	the treatment of this theme by comparing and contrasting the different practices in the three cultures.	

COMPETENCE (In order to ...	PRODUCT/PERFORMANCE ... do what?)	QUALITY CRITERIA ("Look fors")
Produce by ... designing and developing	a written and oral presentation of your findings and conclusion.	• Organize all information in logical, sequential manner. • Clearly and accurately convey the information and your conclusion using standards of grammatical writing.

COMPETENCE	AUDIENCE / SETTING (To/for whom? Where?)	QUALITY CRITERIA ("Look fors")
Disseminate by ... presenting	to a local lawyers' association and/or 10th-grade government class.	• Include appropriate visuals. • Clearly convey message. • React appropriately to audience.

SAMPLE PERFORMANCE DESIGNER FOR GRADE 3

PURPOSE:	LANGUAGE ARTS:
To convey an important message	SPEAKING (SEE PAGE 26)

KEY ORGANIZING QUESTION:

How can you use a skit to convey an important message?

ROLE: *(You are ...)*

A producer

(Who is expected to ...)

COMPETENCE (Do what?)	CONTENT/CONCEPTS (With what?)	QUALITY CRITERIA ("Look fors")
Access and interpret by ... collecting reviewing and selecting	important information on the dangers of using drugs, all of the collected information, the key ideas.	• Identify your purpose. • Select from a variety of resources. • Read and discuss the materials with your team. • Identify the important points.

COMPETENCE (In order to ...	PRODUCT/PERFORMANCE ... do what?)	QUALITY CRITERIA ("Look fors")
Produce by ... developing and designing and creating	the script the necessary props, scenery, and costumes.	• Review the possibilities. • Select your focus. • Identify your beginning, middle, and ending. • Identify only necessary props, simple scenery, and costumes. • Collect and make the essentials.

COMPETENCE	AUDIENCE / SETTING (To/for whom? Where?)	QUALITY CRITERIA ("Look fors")
Disseminate by ... presenting	your skit to another class.	• Speak clearly. • Engage your audience. • Assess the response from your audience.

SAMPLE PERFORMANCE DESIGNER FOR GRADE 5

PURPOSE:
To present a convincing message

**LANGUAGE ARTS:
VIEWING AND REPRESENTING
(SEE PAGE 50)**

KEY ORGANIZING QUESTION:
How do the method and text in a message influence the audience?

ROLE: *(You are ...)*
A designer

(Who is expected to ...)

COMPETENCE (Do what?)	CONTENT/CONCEPTS (With what?)	QUALITY CRITERIA ("Look fors")
Access and interpret by ... observing and analyzing	the text of several popular media messages these messages to learn the different strategies.	• Identify your purpose. • Select a variety of media messages. • Note the different strategies. • Identify the details. • Record your observations.

COMPETENCE (In order to ...	PRODUCT/PERFORMANCE ... do what?)	QUALITY CRITERIA ("Look fors")
Produce by ... designing and creating	a commercial for a particular audience using a specific technique for that audience.	• Select your audience. • Choose your technique. • Develop a draft. • Test your idea. • Represent your idea using appropriate materials.

COMPETENCE	AUDIENCE / SETTING (To/for whom? Where?)	QUALITY CRITERIA ("Look fors")
Disseminate by ... presenting and surveying	your commercial to your identified audience the audience to learn their response to your commercials.	• Arrange with your audience for the viewing. • Conduct the presentation. • Design a survey instrument. • Review its focus. • Print the survey. • Distribute to your audience. • Compute the results.

SAMPLE PERFORMANCE DESIGNER GRADE 8

PURPOSE:	LANGUAGE ARTS:
To identify the techniques of persuasion	VIEWING AND REPRESENTING (SEE PAGE 51)

KEY ORGANIZING QUESTION:
How can a producer influence the emotions and response of the viewer?

ROLE: *(You are ...)*
A publisher

(Who is expected to ...)

COMPETENCE (Do what?)	CONTENT/CONCEPTS (With what?)	QUALITY CRITERIA ("Look fors")
Access and interpret by ... researching	the techniques and strategies used in advertising to entice consumers	• Identify your purpose. • Use a variety of resources. • Organize your information. • Select the most appropriate information. • Prioritize the ideas.
and analyzing	this information.	

COMPETENCE (In order to ...	PRODUCT/PERFORMANCE ... do what?)	QUALITY CRITERIA ("Look fors")
Produce by ... designing	a pamphlet for consumers on advertising techniques	• Identify major purpose. • Select key ideas. • Create a layout. • Review the layout. • Expand necessary details. • Create the final draft.
and developing	your pamphlet.	

COMPETENCE	AUDIENCE / SETTING (To/for whom? Where?)	QUALITY CRITERIA ("Look fors")
Disseminate by ... publishing and distributing	your pamphlet to community members.	• Format the information. • Organize the layout. • Print the pamphlet. • Identify distribution procedures. • Deliver the pamphlet.

SAMPLE PERFORMANCE DESIGNER FOR GRADE 12

PURPOSE:

To draw a conclusion

LANGUAGE ARTS:
VIEWING AND REPRESENTING
(SEE PAGE 52)

KEY ORGANIZING QUESTION:

What effect can sponsors have on issues and positions taken in some media texts?

ROLE: *(You are ...)*

A producer

(Who is expected to ...)

COMPETENCE (Do what?)	CONTENT/CONCEPTS (With what?)	QUALITY CRITERIA ("Look fors")
Access and interpret by ... interviewing and gathering and analyzing	information from several representatives from advertising firms to learn all you can on expectations from financial sponsors or clients on media content the gathered data and draw conclusions.	• Establish clear goals. • Prepare precise questions. • Collect information from a variety of sources. • Document pertinent data. • Select the most important data. • Organize according to your goals.

COMPETENCE (In order to ...	PRODUCT/PERFORMANCE ... do what?)	QUALITY CRITERIA ("Look fors")
Produce by ... laying out and developing	a documentary on how your findings would affect a media producer.	• Identify purpose and audience. • Select appropriate information and examples. • Create a storyboard. • Arrange the ideas and details. • Expand the content. • Record the documentary.

COMPETENCE	AUDIENCE / SETTING (To/for whom? Where?)	QUALITY CRITERIA ("Look fors")
Disseminate by ... broadcasting and evaluating	the documentary to your selected audience the audience response.	• Arrange the details. • Organize the event. • Revisit the experiences. • Identify possible new directions or additions.

APPENDIX: BLANK TEMPLATES

PERFORMANCE DESIGNER

PURPOSE:

- -

KEY ORGANIZING QUESTION:

- -

ROLE: *(You are ...)*

(Who is expected to ...)

COMPETENCE (Do what?)	CONTENT/CONCEPTS (With what?)	QUALITY CRITERIA ("Look fors")
Access and interpret by ...		

COMPETENCE (In order to ...	PRODUCT/PERFORMANCE ... do what?)	QUALITY CRITERIA ("Look fors")
Produce by ...		

COMPETENCE	AUDIENCE / SETTING (To/for whom? Where?)	QUALITY CRITERIA ("Look fors")
Disseminate by ...		

Language Arts:
Grade ___

Performance
Benchmark

CONTENT/CONCEPT STANDARD ___
_____

KEY ORGANIZING QUESTION:

KEY COMPETENCES	KEY CONCEPTS AND CONTENT	PERFORMANCE TASKS
		PERFORMANCE TASK I:
		PERFORMANCE TASK II:

QUALITY CRITERIA:

Technology Connections
_____: Grade ___

Performance
Benchmark

KEY ORGANIZING QUESTION:

ACCESS	PRODUCE	DISSEMINATE
PERFORMANCE TASK I:	**PERFORMANCE TASK I:**	**PERFORMANCE TASK I:**
PERFORMANCE TASK II:	**PERFORMANCE TASK II:**	**PERFORMANCE TASK II:**

BIBLIOGRAPHY

Anderson, R. C., & Chase, R. (1984). *Becoming a nation of readers: The report of the Commission on Reading.* Washington, DC: National Academy of Education, U.S. Department of Education.

Applebee, A. N. (1989). *The teaching of literature in programs with reputations for excellence* (Report Series 1.1). Albany: State University of New York at Albany Center for the Learning and Teaching of Literature.

Arizona State Department of Education. (1990). *Arizona literature essential skills.* Tuscon, AZ: Author.

Atwell, N. (1987). *In the middle: Writing, reading, and learning with adolescents.* Montclair, NJ: Boynton/Cook.

Black, H., & Black, S. (1986). *Building thinking skills.* Pacific Grove, CA: Midwest.

Boyer, E. L. (1983). *High school: A report on secondary education in America.* New York: Harper & Row.

Brandt, R. (Ed.) (1988). *Content of the curriculum: ASCD yearbook.* Alexandria, VA: Association for Supervision and Curriculum Development.

Busching, B., & Schwartz, J. (1984). *Integrating the language arts in the elementary school.* Urbana, IL: National Council of Teachers of English.

California Department of Education. (1986). *Beyond language: Social and cultural factors in schooling language minority students.* Los Angeles: Evaluation, Dissemination and Assessment Center, California State University, Los Angeles.

California Department of Education. (1987). *English language arts framework.* Sacramento, CA: Author.

Calkins, L. M. (1986). *The art of teaching writing.* Portsmouth, NH: Heinemann.

Calkins, L. M. (1991). *Living between the lines.* Portsmouth, NH: Heinemann.

Carnegie Council on Adolescent Development: Task Force on the Education of Young Adolescents. (1989). *Turning points: Preparing American youth for the 21st century.* Washington DC: Author.

Chomsky, N. (1975). *Reflections on language.* New York: Pantheon.

Coburn, P. (1982). *Practical guide to computers in education.* Reading, MA: Addison-Wesley.

Colorado Department of Education. (1986). *Performance-based assessment resource guide.* Denver. CO: Author.

Commission on the Teaching Profession. (1985). *Who will teach our children?: A strategy for improving California's schools.* Sacramento, CA: Author.

Cooper, D. (1993). *Literacy: Helping children construct meaning.* Boston, MA: Houghton Mifflin.

Copperman, P. (1978). *The literary hoax: The decline of reading, writing and learning in the public schools and what we can do about it.* New York: William Morrow.

Curry, B., & Temple, J. (1992). *Using curriculum frameworks for systemic reform.* Alexandria, VA: Association for Supervision and Curriculum Development.

Downey, C. J. (1991). *Curriculum design and delivery.* Temple, AZ: Kyrene School District.

Durkin, D. (1978). What classroom observations reveal about comprehension. *Reading Research Quarterly, 14*(4), 481-533.

Easton, L. B. (1991). *Developing educational performance tests for a statewide program: Educational performance assessment.* Chicago: Riverside.

Edelshy, C., Altwerger, B., & Flores, B. (1991). *Whole language: What's the difference?* Portsmouth, NH: Heinemann.

Diegmueller, K., Olson, L., Viadero, D., & Lasoff, M. (1995, April 12). Struggling for standards, a special report. *Education Week,* pp. 1-70.

Fancher, R., Finn, C. Jr., & Ravitch, D. (Eds.) (1984). *Against mediocrity: The humanities in America's high schools.* New York: Holmes & Meier.

Fisher, B. (1991). *Joyful learning.* Portsmouth, NH: Heinemann.

Fogarty, R. (1991). *The mindful schools: How to integrate the curricula.* Paladne, IL: Skylight.

Fulwiler, T., & Young, A. (Eds.) (1982). *Language connections.* Urbana, IL: National Council of Teachers of English.

Goodlad, J. (1984). *A place called school: Prospects for the future.* New York: McGraw-Hill.

Goodman, K. S. (1986). *What's whole in whole language?* Portsmouth, NH: Heinemann.

Hansen, J., Graves, D., & Newkirk, T. (Eds.) (1985). *Breaking ground: Teachers relate reading and writing in the elementary school.* Portsmouth, NH: Heinemann.

Harste, J. C. (1989). *New policy guidelines for reading: Connecting research and practice.* Urbana, IL: National Council of Teachers of English.

Heide, A., & Henderson, D. (1994). *The technological classroom: A blueprint for success.* Toronto, Canada: Trefolium.

Hirsch, E. D.,Jr. (Spring, 1983). Cultural literacy. *The American Scholar, 52*(2), 159-69.

Idaho State Department of Education. (1990). *Integrated language arts course of study, K-8.* Boise, ID: Author.

Jacobs, H. H. (1989). Design options for an integrated curriculum. In H. H. Jacobs (Ed.), *Interdisciplinary Curriculum Design and Implementation,* pp. 13-24. Alexandria, VA: Association for Supervision and Curriculum Development.

Langer, J. A., & Applebee, A. N. (1987). *How writing shapes thinking.* Urbana, IL: National Council of Teachers of English.

Manning, M. A., Manning, G., & Wartman, B. (1991). A glossary of whole language terms. *Teaching K-8, 22,* 54-56.

Maryland State Department of Education. (1987). *English language arts: A Maryland curricular framework.* Baltimore, MD: Author.

Marzano. R. J., (1992a). *A different kind of classroom.* Alexandria, VA: Association for Supervision and Curriculum Development.

Marzano. R. J. (1992b). *Dimensions of thinking: A framework for curriculum and instruction.* Alexandria, VA: Association for Supervision and Curriculum Development.

Mayhew, J., Lester, N., & Pradi, G. (1983) *Learning to write, writing to learn.* Portsmouth, NH: Boynton/Cook.

McClain, L. (1981). Study guides: Potential assets in content classrooms. *Journal of Reading, 24,* 321-325.

McElhaney, R. (1994). Standards for the assessment of reading and writing. Newark, DE: National Council of Teachers of English.

Michigan State Board of Education. (1991). *Model core curriculum outcomes and position statement on core curriculum.* Lansing, MI: Author.

Michigan State Board of Education. (1994a). *Core curriculum content standards and benchmarks for scademic content standards for English language arts.* Draft. Lansing, MI: Author.

Michigan State Board of Education. (1994b). *Michigan high school proficiency test in communication arts.* Lansing, MI: Author.

Minnesota Department of Education. (1982). *Some essential learner outcomes in communications/language arts.* St. Paul, MN: Author.

Moffett, J., & Wagner, B. J. (1976). *Student-centered language arts and reading, K-13.* Boston, MA: Houghton Mifflin.

National Commission on Excellence in Education. (1983). *A nation at risk: The imperative for educational reform.* Washington, DC: U.S. Department of Education.

National Council of Teachers of English. (1983). *The essentials of English.* Urbana, IL: Author.

National Council of Teachers of English. (1986). *Activities to promote critical thinking.* Urbana, IL: NCTE Committee on Classroom Practices in Teaching English.

Norton, D. E. (1990). Teaching multicultural literature in the reading curriculum. *The Reading Teacher, 44*(1), 28.

Ogle, D. (1986). K-W-L: A teaching model that develops a reading of expository text. *The Reading Teacher, 39,* 564-570.

Ontario Ministry of Education and Training. (1995). *The common curriculum, provincial standards, language.* Ottawa, Ontario, Canada: Author.

Parry, J. A., & Hornsby, D. (1985). *Write on: A conference approach to writing.* Portsmouth, NH: Heinemann.

Perrone, V. (1991). *Expanding student assessment.* Alexandria, VA: Association for Supervision and Curriculum Development.

Purves, A., & the Task Force on Measurement and Evaluation in the Study of English. (1975). *Common sense and testing in English.* Urbana, IL: National Council of Teachers of English.

Resnick, L., & Klopfer, M. (Eds.) (1989). *Toward the thinking curriculum: Overview. Association for Supervision and Curriculum Development Yearbook.* Alexandria, VA: Association for the Development of Supervision and Curriculum Development.

Romano, T. (1987). *Clearing the way: Working with teenage writers.* Portsmouth, NH: Heinemann.

Rosenblatt, L. (1978). *The reader, the text, the poem: The transactional theory of the literary work.* Urbana, IL: National Council Teachers of English.

Routman, R. (1988). *Transitions: From literature to literacy.* Portsmouth, NH: Heinemann.

Routman, R. (1991). *Invitations: Changing teachers and learners, K-12.* Portsmouth, NH: Heinemann.

Smith, E. B., Goodman, K., & Meredith, R. (1976). *Language and thinking in school* (2nd ed.). New York: Holt, Rinehart, & Winston.

Spady, W. B., & Marshall, K. J. (1991). Beyond traditional outcome-based education. *Educational Leadership, 49*(2), 67-72.

Speech Communication Association. (1982a). *Essential speaking and listening competencies for high school graduates.* Annandale, VA: Author.

Speech Communication Association. (1982b). *Essential speaking and listening skills for elementary school students* (6th-grade level). Annandale, VA: Author.

Squire, J. (Ed.) (1977). *The teaching of English: The 76th yearbook of the National Society for the Study of Education.* Chicago: University of Chicago Press.

Stewig, J. W., & Sebesta, S. L. (1978). *Using literature in the elementary classroom.* Urbana, IL: National Council of Teachers of English.

Tarleton, R. (1988). *Learning and talking: A practical guide to oracy across the curriculum.* London: Routledge.

Tchudi, S. (1991). *Planning and assessing the curriculum in English language arts.* Alexandria, VA: Association for Supervision and Curriculum Development.

Thaiss, C. (1986). *Language across the curriculum in the elementary grades.* Urbana, IL: National Council of Teachers of English.

Tierney, R. J., Carter, M. A., & Desai, L. E. (1991). *Portfolio assessment in the reading-writing classroom.* Norwood, MA: Christopher-Gordon.

Tye, K. A. (Ed.) (1991) *Global education: Yearbook of the Association for Supervision and Curriculum Development.* Alexandria, VA: Association for Supervision and Curriculum Development.

University of California, Los Angeles. (1985). *Literature for all students.* Los Angeles, CA: Author.

Valencia, S. W. (1990). A portfolio approach to classroom reading assessment: The whys, whats, and hows. *The Reading Teacher, 43*, 338-340.

Wilkinson, A. (1970). The concept of oracy. *English Journal. 59*(1), 71-77.

Wisconsin Department of Public Instruction. (1990). *A guide to curriculum planning in classroom drama and theater.* Madison, WI: Author.

Wolf, D. P. (1988). *Reading reconsided: Literature and literacy in high school.* Albany, NY: New York College Entrance Examination Board.

Wresch, W. (Ed.) (1991). *The English classroom in the computer age.* Urbana, IL: National Council of Teachers of English.

CORWIN
PRESS

The Corwin Press logo — a raven striding across an open book — represents the happy union of courage and learning. We are a professional-level publisher of books and journals for K-12 educators, and we are committed to creating and providing resources that embody these qualities. Corwin's motto is "Success for All Learners."